Faculty Recruitment, Retention, and Fair Employment:
Obligations and Opportunities

by John S. Waggaman

ASHE-ERIC/Higher Education Research Report No. 2, 1983

Prepared by

® *Clearinghouse on Higher Education*
The George Washington University

Published by

Association for the Study of Higher Education

Jonathan D. Fife,
Series Editor

Cite as:
Waggaman, John S. *Faculty Recruitment, Retention, and Fair Employment: Obligations and Opportunities*. ASHE-ERIC/Higher Education Research Report No. 2. Washington, D.C.: Association for the Study of Higher Education, 1983.

The Eric Clearinghouse on Higher Education invites individuals to submit proposals for writing monographs for the Higher Education Research Report series. Proposals must include:
1. A detailed manuscript proposal of not more than five pages.
2. A 75-word summary to be used by several review committees for the initial screening and rating of each proposal.
3. A vita.
4. A writing sample.

ISSN 0737-1292

ERIC* Clearinghouse on Higher Education
The George Washington University
One Dupont Circle, Suite 630
Washington, D.C. 20036

Association for the Study of Higher Education
One Dupont Circle, Suite 630
Washington, D.C. 20036

This publication was prepared with funding from the National Institute of Education, U.S. Department of Education, under contract no. 400-82-0011. The opinion expressed in this report do not necessarily reflect the positions or policies of NIE or the Department.

CONTENTS

FOREWORD

The conditions facing faculty employment make it both a buyer's and a seller's market. On the one hand, there are academic areas where faculty are in high demand by industry and are being enticed away from academe by offers of high salaries and fringe benefits. On the other, academic areas with low turnover and a limited number of new job openings make it a buyer's market. In either case, it is now more important than ever for higher education institutions to carefully review their policies and practices concerning faculty employment.

One reason for the need for reexamination is that the recruitment process is expensive. The direct costs are varied: advertising position openings, travel expenses to interview candidates, and moving expenses for new hires. Equally expensive are the indirect costs to the university as faculty and support staff lose time from their normal duties to serve on search committees, review resumes, and interview candidates.

Psychological as well as economic aspects of faculty employment are equally important. Each new faculty member plays a significant role in the overall quality and dynamics of an institution. A stagnant faculty makes a stagnant institution. When higher education was expanding, there was a constant flow of new ideas, opinions, and state-of-the-art skills. Today in academic areas with low turnover and no growth, an increasing percentage of the faculty is tenured, resulting in limited interjection of new ideas. Therefore, new faculty play an increasingly important role in stimulating intellectual dynamics in an academic area.

Additionally, for tenured track positions in areas of low turnover, it is important to consider future as well as present needs. Institutions can no longer assume that when new skills are needed new faculty will be hired. Search committees should try to anticipate the skills needed 10 or 15 years from now and to avoid the difficult task of later having to correct a wrong hiring decision.

Race and sex discrimination and the desire to remedy past imbalances make hiring decisions even more difficult with low turnover. Institutions whose objectives are to develop a balanced faculty must be concerned with their hiring practices in order to avoid being accused of reverse discrimination.

Finally, institutions must also become aware of the importance of retaining quality faculty. Under current conditions it is not unlikely that high quality faculty will be recruited by other institutions or industry, while lower quality faculty will remain. It is also probable that it will be the faculty of high confidence or creativity who will voluntarily leave the institution first.

In this report by John S. Waggaman, Associate Professor, College of Education, Florida State University, the recruitment process is reviewed thoroughly. He highlights the steps involved in preliminary planning, organizing recruitment, screening applicants' files, the campus visit, and final decisions, and also reviews the steps to be considered in retaining new faculty. The model developed by Dr. Waggaman will be very useful as institutions and academic departments refine their faculty recruitment practices.

Jonathan D. Fife
Director and Series Editor
[ERIC]* Clearinghouse on Higher Education
The George Washington University

EXECUTIVE SUMMARY

Faculty Recruitment, Retention and Fair Employment: Obligations and Opportunities examines the central issues and processes of recruiting and retaining faculty in the context of managing human resources and the principles of fair employment. It focuses on the needs of department or division heads, but it would be useful to any college or university administrator with responsibility for recruiting faculty. The department or division chair can blend the following procedures into the policies and practices of any institution. Although a small department might be able to recruit faculty in a much less detailed manner than outlined in the report, it is still likely to face the same issues and problems.

The report is organized by the stages of the recruitment process: receiving notification of a vacant position, receiving the authorization to recruit, determining salary, organizing the recruitment effort, screening applicants' files, conducting campus visits, and making an offer. It concludes with the factors needed to retain qualified faculty: orientation, professional development, periodic counseling, and mentorship.

Why Is Recruitment Important Now?

The central focus of the report is recruitment, but serious recruitment without an awareness of the factors that encourage faculty to stay once hired could result in wasted effort. Both the department and the candidates could be losers (DuVall 1976). An effective recruiting program is one that locates the best candidate available, who is made an acceptable job offer and then stays in the department 8 or more years, developing a productive career and benefiting both the institution and himself. The report recognizes the hard new realities of academic employment:

> There simply aren't going to be position openings to advance all our causes. We can't support a steadily aging tenured faculty and extend the retirement age and create many opportunities for younger minorities and women faculty at the same time (Linnell 1979, p. 1).

Clearly, recruiting faculty is not going to become any easier. Each vacancy that occurs in the early 1980s may be the last one for a long time (Fernandez 1978; National Science Foundation 1981). Linnell reports the possibility of only 6,400 new doctoral positions per year from 1983 through 1998, plus a

Serious recruitment without an awareness of the factors that encourage faculty to stay once hired could result in wasted effort.

---

much larger "churning" of nontenured faculty between institutions (1979, p. 5). The new Ph.D.s in this latter group have been termed "gypsy scholars," indicating that they will take almost any academic appointment, anywhere, for whatever duration (Hechinger 1982; Yarrow 1982). Department heads and other academic administrators need to be especially open and forthright with these people, whether they are hired for full-time, part-time, or temporary positions.

Successful recruiting results from a department chair's commitment to people-oriented administration. The chair must collect information about the career status of each faculty member to be able to estimate retirement dates and other conditions that project the future need for faculty. Plans can therefore be made before the need to hire new faculty arises, and principles of affirmative action can be made part of those plans.

Planning for What?
Vacancies open for many reasons—an institution's desire to maintain a fixed student-faculty ratio, demographic and market changes, retirement, involuntary separation, refusal of promotion and tenure, incompetence, moral turpitude, contract termination without prejudice, voluntary separation, departure by mutual consent, disability, and death. A chair who understands the career paths of faculty can understand and even predict likely changes in the department's instructional staff. These changes provide many opportunities to reshape a department, and they may be as important as recruiting new faculty. For example, a chair might face pressure from women, minorities, and gypsy scholars to remove incompetent faculty to make way for the next generation of faculty.

Planning the recruitment program involves several steps. Usually a dean must approve the decision to hire a new person before any action can be taken. The position must be reviewed so that its next occupant meets the needs of the college and the department. Institutional policies must be examined, affirmative action guidelines reviewed, and decisions made about any special efforts to recruit minorities and women. A department may have to show evidence of its commitment to equal employment opportunity, including goals, timetables, and written plans to contact sources of potential applicants. The salary for the position should be reviewed; it may be possible to hire part-time faculty or to create two positions when the vacant position was filled by a highly paid faculty member. Reviewing the salary also allows the institution to ensure that salaries are equitable regardless of the new member's race or sex.

The department chair should appoint a search committee to recruit new faculty. The search committee can define the professional characteristics each candidate should have. It must establish policies (within institutional guidelines) about special cases—the criteria for ineligibility, nepotism, hiring alumni, late applicants, for example. The committee can prepare an announcement of the available position and decide where to send the information. Arrangements need to be made for setting up applicants' files and interview records, confirming data about race and sex, and so on.

How Should We Sift, Weigh, and Judge?

Once the closing date is past, each applicant's file must be screened, first to determine which ones do not comply with the institution's and the department's recruitment policies. Those applicants who were given some preferential attention should be noted and then treated no differently from other applicants. A second review of applicants' files should determine those whose applications conform to the advertised requirements for the position. The applicants who barely missed being declared eligible should be identified and retained for one more evaluation. This surviving group—all those who are eligible plus the marginal applicants—should now be considered nominees, and the search committee should rank the most outstanding nominees. The final group of three to five applicants become the candidates for the position.

The department chair and the search committee next begin a final round of telephone checks of references and credentials. The dean must approve bringing some or all of the candidates to the campus for personal interviews. The chair can begin negotiations with the candidates over the telephone, clearing up any questions and extending an invitation to visit the campus, deliver a lecture, and meet with faculty and administrators. All those who talk to the candidates should then evaluate them. The data for each candidate are complied and presented in aggregate form to the search committee, which recommends the best candidates to the department head. After conferring with the dean, the department chair offers the position to the best candidate. The records of the search must be retained for 3 years.

What Are Fair Procedures?

The content and form of the announcements of the vacancy must be fairly presented. All persons interested in a position should be given the same set of instructions for submitting a complete application. Applicants known to the faculty should be identified; if they are said to have special qualities not sought in the announcement, all applicants should be surveyed for those qualities.

A department wishing to change the percentage of its faculty who are minorities or women can do several things: It can decide and publish the most desirable goal for percentages; it can determine the geographic origins of its faculty and students and decide where it would be appropriate to recruit new faculty; it can prepare a plan with dates for achieving major goals; it can keep adequate records showing the efforts made to seek out applicants. Institutions with affirmative action plans can provide guidelines for departments; otherwise, a department must make its own commitment and carry it out.

After Recruitment, What?

The fair procedures and due process to be observed are part of a sound program of managing talent. The procedures require that faculty be consulted regularly, that jointly negotiated assignments be determined, that criteria and methods of evaluating faculty be made explicit, and that each faculty member have an opportunity to participate in a continuing professional development program. Counseling to help faculty correct deficiencies and opportunities to develop needed skills should be available. All expectations for performance must be made explicit, and each faculty member must be given an adequate chance to develop professionally.

Recruiting is only the first step; keeping faculty is another matter. After their arrival, faculty need to be apprised of the formal terms of the contractual relationship. The department head is largely responsible for designing development programs that will aid new faculty to become successful professionals. Formal orientation and career counseling can help new faculty understand how decisions are made in the department and institution. Established faculty and their spouses can help newcomers adjust to the new community.

A chair would do well to understand why one person might accept a job offer and another would turn it down. He can benefit by knowing why faculty move to other institutions. A department chair should consider the concept of mentorship, particularly for women and minorities. With the appropriate planning and sensitivity, a department can recruit fairly from among all races and both sexes and build a quality faculty.

Declining enrollments, dwindling budgets, fewer available vacancies, and the necessity to exhibit affirmative action in recruiting new faculty make the chair's role a challenging one.

The department chair is an administrator and leader whose resources are individuals. His roles include conservator and developer of human beings, leader in evaluating the productivity and quality of faculty work, and planner who must decide when to strengthen the department's resources by identifying incompetent faculty. In all these roles, the department chair must exhibit absolute fairness, administered with the wisdom of Solomon. And these days of declining enrollments, dwindling budgets, fewer available vacancies, and the necessity to exhibit affirmative action in recruiting new faculty make the chair's role even more challenging.

Recruiting faculty should not be ad hoc (Smelser and Content 1980). A department chair can estimate when many, perhaps 75 percent, of all vacancies will occur many months or years before faculty actually leave the department. An inventory of information about departmental faculty—carefully maintained files about faculty members—can help the chair systematically estimate potential departure dates. To reliably estimate the dates when vacancies are likely to occur requires the chair to understand thoroughly the variety of circumstances that precede the departure of faculty, the emergence of a vacancy, or the approval of a new position.

Vacancies arise for many reasons: institutional policies and practices, demographic changes, changes in the job market, retirement, involuntary separation, decisions not to promote or grant tenure to faculty, incompetence, contract termination, voluntary separation, departure by mutual agreement, and disability or death (Linnell 1979).* The chair who wants to add younger people, women, or minorities to the faculty may find his only option is to consider involuntary or mutually agreed upon separation for demonstrated incompetence as the principal means by which vacancies will develop. In that case, however, the chair must ensure faculty are treated fairly by using processes to make professional assignments, aid in the development of faculty, and evaluate performance *before* it is decided to terminate faculty. These systematic processes are the chair's primary management tools, for they give faculty a fair opportunity to develop, improve, and perform appropriately. They

*While this section focuses on the circumstances that cause vacancies to arise, it is not meant to imply that the chair should strive to *create* vacancies.

should be the principal sources of evidence—and the only fair way—to varify competence.

Academic policies are not often examined for their effect on the availability of faculty positions, but they can play an important role. For example, an institution or department that operates with a relatively stable student-faculty ratio has a de facto policy on the establishment of new positions, which often becomes obvious only when circumstances change. Its existence and impact is made explicit only when a faculty member leaves a position and a decision must be made about refilling the position or when student enrollments increase and new faculty positions are necessary to keep the ratio intact. When enrollments decline, the institution might then look for ways to redesign policies and programs to increase enrollments, perhaps by attracting new clientele. Usually the last consideration is reducing faculty, yet that step might be necessary if demographic changes signal a long-term decline.

The institution that can afford it may not reduce faculty positions when enrollments decline but instead commit itself to systematically reducing the student-faculty ratio (Gaddy 1969). For many institutions, however, this luxury is beyond reach because institutions with professional programs might find that their professional associations demand a small student-faculty ratio. A department chair who would like to follow professional standards but also must compete for resources in a financially anemic institution might find it necessary to seek external funding for the continuation of existing positions or for the funding of new positions.

Planning
The chair who wants to add a position to the existing departmental faculty needs to become involved in long-range planning. Analysis of past departmental enrollments, future demand for graduates, and potential future enrollments, is a necessity. While institutional officials tend to resist the creation of new full-time positions whenever a department experiences a relatively short-term increase in enrollment, most officials are willing to be convinced of the need for new faculty if enrollment in a department continues to grow.

Typically, a department chair does not have access to sufficient or appropriate kinds of planning data. The institutional research, planning, and/or budget office may be helpful in supplying the data; city, regional, state, or other planning officials may be able to supply the appropriate market demand data. A small faculty committee could be formed to assemble the information. Its search could be the beginning of continuous departmental planning, especially important for departments whose head changes every few years.

One planning task for which the chair must be responsible is the personnel inventory, which represents an explicit effort to assess the stability of faculty and staff in the department. A complete inventory would identify faculty competencies and interests, relating them to the courses being taught and the subject areas most often chosen for research and development projects. With such an inventory, the chair can see which areas of specialization are under- or overstaffed, which current areas remain uncovered, and which are unaddressed. Based on the data compiled, the chair can realistically assess the strengths of the department's specialties. Overstaffed or mediocre-to-poor quality specialty areas or newly emerging "hot" areas are revealed. This information makes it possible to suggest retraining for new specialties rather than laying off faculty. It also helps justify the need for new positions.

Vacancies Resulting from Retirement

The personnel inventory must also include an estimate of when each faculty member is likely to leave the department. Obviously, the chair must be well informed about the career status of each faculty member. The most factual element in this data set is retirement dates, but they have become less fixed recently. Some faculty have chosen early retirement and others have elected later retirement.

While the normal retirement age is usually thought of as 65, some senior faculty have chosen early retirement at age 62. The ravages of inflation on the purchasing power of the typical retirement income, however, have encouraged an increasing number of faculty to stay until age 70. Senior faculty can recall with a shudder the painful circumstances of the 1930s, when most faculty had no retirement benefits and worked in shredded cuffs until death terminated their employment. The horrors of a penurious retirement, whether forced or voluntary, can be reduced only by institutional administrators, government policies, and personal financial planning. A department chair can be of some assistance by helping retiring faculty develop part-time teaching jobs. Several states and higher education systems permit retirement after 30 years of service (or service time purchased to equal 30 years). This option is an important one for opening vacancies. How to encourage faculty to select this option is a serious challenge to department heads in the 1980s (Linnell 1979).

The department chair has the responsibility to assess the impact of later retirement and an aging faculty on students. Is a younger, more exuberant faculty easier for students to identify with? Or is an older faculty, filled with wisdom and compassion for the young, more attractive to students? The answer appears related not so much to age as to enjoyment of one's career. When faculty—whether senior or middle-aged trying to cope with a mid-life crisis—are bored to death with teaching, are not involved in many, or any, scholarly activities, and relish only a comfortable retirement, they are usually seen as abusing the professional autonomy given faculty when they seem to take early "retirement" while still holding a full-time paying job. A chair should realize that early retirement or involuntary severance of such people is the only way that faculty vacancies might open in the next 10 years. The central issue that the chair must decide is whether to become involved in proposing a program of professional development and evaluation for those colleagues labeled unproductive. There will be few difficulties if the chair can stimulate his or her colleagues to again become productive; for those colleagues who cannot or will not respond positively, the chair's efforts may become the primary evidence in terminating faculty who are performing poorly.

Involuntary Separation
A chair must sort out clearly and fairly the alternatives inherent in an involuntary termination. A number of concerns must be addressed before involuntary separation is a workable choice. First, a department chair must understand that some faculty might perform poorly or be unproductive and that systematic evaluation from the time they are first hired can help substantiate an ultimate decision to terminate. Most chairs with responsibility for a departmental budget are also responsible for helping unproductive faculty through systematic negotiation with the faculty member, agreement on a development program (to be reviewed quarterly), and incorporation of some professional development objectives in the annual and term assignments. The chair must make sure the faculty member knows what is expected, the criteria for evaluation, and how progress

Any attempt to terminate faculty to create vacancies without following the best principles of faculty development and evaluation is sure to engender grievances and court action, with a high likelihood that the chair will lose.

or success will be determined. A faculty committee should pass on the fairness of the individual's development plan and then review the admissible evidence for assessing performance. The overriding purpose of faculty development is to improve performance. The chair must maintain a record of the quality of performance. Poor performance over some fixed period of time will become the evidence upon which the decision to initiate termination procedures is based. This approach to faculty development and separation is fair and humanitarian. It places a high value on changing people's behavior so that their behavior brings them rewards and recognition *and* also supports the goals of the department and institution. Helping to salvage an unproductive faculty member's career may be the greatest challenge a chair will face.

In one form or another, due process procedures *must* be observed before a department can begin termination action. People must have been notified of their unproductive behavior and specifically given the opportunity to become productive. Thus, any attempt to terminate faculty to create vacancies without following the best principles of faculty development and evaluation is sure to engender grievances and court action, with a high likelihood that the chair will lose (see Rood 1977).

Second, procedures for due process rest on the fundamental assumption that individuals should be able to defend themselves against arbitrary and capricious administrative decisions. The procedures at the heart of performance evaluation rest on another important assumption, namely, that colleges and universities are meritocratic systems and should be devoid of discrimination in whatever form. Attempts by chairs (or deans, or anyone else) to force out a person because of personal differences so a vacancy can be created will immediately be subject to the suspicion that their actions are designed to benefit themselves, as an insidious means that was used solely to create an opening for a friend needing a job or to rescue a colleague at another institution or to create a job for a relative. Women and minority applicants for faculty positions often are suspicious that any vacancy, regardless of how it was created, is most often filled by this kind of "patronage," for most of the replacements tend to be white males. Thus, to follow open and specific procedures for removal and appointment is to create a true climate of fairness.

Third, no government regulations require that an institution's or department's administrators must terminate faculty so that vacancies can be created and subsequently filled with women or minority members. While it is true that some universities that exercise strong central control over all faculty and staff positions may manipulate the availability of a vacancy by attempting to withhold announcement of a vacancy until the department finds one or more affirmative action candidates, this action is clearly in violation of the general principles of affirmative action. All vacancies for regular positions must be announced and publicized; and postponing an announcement, like "patronage," is counter to the principles of fair employment.

Faculty may be involuntarily separated for other, more flagrant, reasons involving legal actions resulting from "crimes against society"—a wide range of behaviors from sexual harassment to murder. Vacancies can arise if people are convicted of any of these charges or if they are confronted with sufficient evidence of inappropriate behavior and decide voluntarily to resign rather than face an open hearing or a trial.

Negative Decisions about Promotion and Tenure
Another special kind of involuntary separation, "out" rather than "up," results from the decision to award tenure. It is one of the situations most troublesome to a department chair. The decision not to grant tenure may be preceded by the denial of a request for promotion or other professional award like membership in a graduate faculty. A department chair can identify the "up-or-out" year on the personnel file for each faculty member and realistically estimate the vacancies that could become available as a result of such decisions.

A chair may find the decisions to promote faculty and to grant tenure severely trying. The process should begin with the chair's making a judgment about the fitness of a faculty member to be evaluated. That is, the chair should use the personnel inventory and annual evaluation data to decide whether the faculty member is ready for a faculty review. In conjunction with the faculty member, he should prepare a file with all the appropriate evidence included.

The chair has to discuss the current and future probabilities of success with the faculty member. If he believes the faculty member is unlikely to be recommended by the members of a departmental committee, he should explain that message, with reasons and areas for improvement specified, to the faculty member. At the same session, the chair should suggest activities to be completed that would most likely improve the faculty member's chances for a successful peer review. If the faculty member wants to proceed with a peer review, despite the chair's counsel, he should be permitted to do so. Similarly, a candidate receiving a negative recommendation at any step of the way should have the privilege of completing the entire process or of withdrawing from consideration before a final decision is made.

A chair may face substantial pressures when attempting to assist a candidate who receives negative ratings in an early stage of a peer review. In this situation, the chair must decide whether to present minimal facts supporting such a candidacy or to become an avowed advocate for the candidate. This choice looms large when the candidates are women or minority members and they appear as qualified as some of the current tenured faculty in the department. Recruiting these individuals in accordance with the principles of affirmative action does not require that they be given special dispensation in promotions and tenure, but to recruit them without guiding them toward success is to make a mockery of affirmative action. It also makes human sacrifices of them on the inflated altars of merit and quality. A chair can avoid most of the inhumane trauma by regularly counseling all the untenured and junior faculty. Additionally, a two- or three-person (tenured) faculty guidance committee could be formed to review the achievements of junior faculty. The committee could perform a full-scale but informal evaluation of junior faculty after 2 or 3 years of employment so that the formal promotion or tenure proceedings hold no surprises. The focus should be on counseling and guidance *during* the academic year as well as at the end.

When it becomes clear, however, that a junior faculty member is not likely to survive the system, counseling of a different nature is in order. Generally, after 3 years of employment, a nontenured faculty member must be given 1 year's notice if the institution intends not to renew his contract. All procedures of due process must be closely followed, and the chair would do well to seek expert legal counsel. For example, beginning to recruit a replacement before the person to be replaced has been given official notice might embroil the institution in legal proceedings.

The grievances and court actions being brought against colleges and universities over promotion and tenure seem to be increasing—at least more of them are being reported in the media. Many actions are being brought by women who allege that the criteria for promotion and tenure are unwritten, unclear, and vague and that the requirements are more rigorously applied to them than to other faculty. An objective, explicit, and fair evaluation system can be easily defended in any circumstances. Vague criteria for promotion and tenure may not appear to be a problem for the exceptional scholar, but they do leave much to chance and invite ill-considered judgment and outright bias. Furthermore, they do not provide guidance to the aspiring faculty member, nor do they provide administrators or members of review committees the means for rationally deciding who should be rewarded or found wanting.

State statutes, court decisions, and collective bargaining contract provisions may constrain the department head's actions. Most of such written material protects faculty from arbitrary removal or from being fired without cause. Because most colleges and universities have such poor systems of professional evaluation and development, the tenure and seniority systems in place now equally protect both the productive and the nonproductive faculty.

Contract Termination

Contract terminations result from one of three sets of events. First is the simple ending of the contract with the person leaving in good standing. Under the proper circumstances, the chair would have no qualms about rehiring the individual. Some contracts now contain clauses specifically stating that a position is for a fixed period of time, is nonrenewable, and will not result in the granting of tenure. If contract positions are full-time and appear like those for regular faculty, they may be designed to rotate people through the positions; in such cases a nonrenewal provision should be clearly stated in the contract. Even people appointed in such positions, however, should be evaluated so that the quality of their performance can be reported when references are requested and so that they can learn of their professional strengths and weaknesses. A chair has to be completely open with aspirants about the probability of permanent employment at the end of the contract. To do otherwise is to appear to unfairly exploit these people. Similarly, if a fixed-term contract is renewable, the chair must make that fact clear and must fully reveal the procedures for evaluation. He should make sure the instructor understands the desired performance level to be achieved on each set of evaluation criteria that will be applied. A chair needs to be open and fair in these matters, if for no

other reason than to avoid any unnecessary delays in filling an expired contract position because of charges that improper evaluation procedures were used.

The second form of contract termination involves voluntary separation—the faculty member who leaves the department, with or without advance notice, for another job. The chair should examine carefully the reasons that faculty leave positions. It should be assumed that two sets of factors motivate a mover: (1) the negative factors perceived in the department and/or dissatisfaction with home life, the factors pushing the mover, and (2) the attractiveness of the new position, the factors pulling the mover to a new location.

During the expansion of higher education in the 1960s, it was common to know personally two or three faculty members a year who moved to another institution (Crane 1970). Reasons for leaving included relatively low pay and benefits, low status and perquisites, dictatorial chairs or a closed structure of departmental governance, and limited opportunity. In a multiyear informal survey by this author of faculty who left a large midwestern state university, it appeared that over half of the faculty turnover was the result of spouses' dissatisfaction. Many wives were isolated in houses in suburban neighborhoods, with young children, a large mortgage, and probably only one car in the family. All her friends and relatives, the people who could provide moral support, were left behind. The husband was most often untenured and worked all hours of the day and night, seven days a week, in pursuit of teaching, research, and publication. When the chance for advancement grew unpromising and life at home became untenable, many of these people sought employment closer to "home," i.e., nearer to her family or his or to institutions where graduate school colleagues were employed.

Even though life styles of younger faculty have changed, it seems abundantly clear that new faculty members coming to an institution that is a long way from family and friends need a local support network. The wives of faculty members have recognized this need and acted positively to integrate newcomers into the college and community, but the more competitive and autonomous a faculty is, the less likelihood such support systems will develop. In any event, a chair should be extra sensitive to the fact that recruitment is only the first step in building a faculty; keeping one is a continuing part of the job. Finding the right candidate after a long search, then losing the person a

Finding the right candidate after a long search, then losing the person a few years later when he or she moves back home is a very ineffective strategy of faculty development.

few years later when he moves back home is a very ineffective strategy of faculty development.

The chair should become sensitive to situations where a faculty member exhibits continued depression, hostility, or open disaffection with the department. If they appear on the verge of becoming alienated from most of their colleagues, the chair may want to counsel the faculty member to seek employment elsewhere, perhaps even assist the person to locate another position. It may be the humane course of action because the person may be basically competent and productive but unable to function well in a particular location, poisoning the morale of and relationships with other faculty, staff, or students. The chair should consult with senior faculty and other administrative officers before undertaking this kind of action so as not to breach any codes of ethics or contracts. And he should scrupulously avoid the appearance of trying to get rid of someone.

The third set of circumstances resulting in contract termination involves mutual agreement between a faculty member and institutional administrators. Faculty members who correctly perceive their inability to survive peer review for promotion or tenure may leave before their up-or-out year. Unproductive tenured faculty members may leave the institution voluntarily after being warned to act more responsibly or face disciplinary action and possible termination. Other faculty may elect to leave voluntarily after being confronted with charges or evidence of unethical actions. In such instances, the chair's role is not to threaten a faculty member with dismissal but to explain that certain kinds of behavior are subject to formal inquiry that may result in a recommendation of dismissal. In no event should the chair act unilaterally; he should take these actions only after consulting with the appropriate institutional officials. Any attempts to confront faculty or staff with their alleged wrongdoings only to observe their reactions and get them to resign voluntarily can only be seen as an administrator's attempt to intimidate the alleged culprit. Such actions violate all normal rights of due process for the accused, are enormously unjust to the innocent, and may result in extended grievances and legal proceedings, leaving the chair unable to do anything about the position or its current occupant. Thus, a longer formal inquiry may be the shorter procedure in the long run. It is best to fully and formally document every personnel action and seek expert guidance and counsel about unusual cases.

Disability or Death

The disability or death of a faculty member requires special attention. If the disability is not permanent, a decision must be made about obtaining a replacement or doubling up the teaching assignments of other department faculty. If no funds are available to hire a temporary replacement, doubling up or canceling some classes may be necessary.

A permanent disability often is determined after 3 to 6 months of treatment and confinement. Only in rare instances is a chair likely to be able to anticipate such a situation, although persons who are chronic smokers and drinkers should be seen as candidates for a serious illness. Once a person is declared permanently disabled, he is usually transferred from a departmental budget to another pay category. When that transfer is made, the remaining salary funds can be used to hire temporary part-time or full-time replacements. It may be necessary to take emergency action to fill the vacancy. Even in an emergency, however, the vacancy should be filled only with a temporary person, pending a formal search. The temporary occupant may be a candidate for the position, but the department chair and the search committee must ensure that an objective search is undertaken. A department that often uses part-time instructors might develop a policy stating that people who are professionally qualified and evaluated favorably on part-time assignments may be advanced to nominee status if they are interested in a full-time position. A predetermined policy of this kind can help remove suspicions of patronage when positions must be filled under these circumstances. Such candidates' files should contain the usual materials plus a copy of the policy statement.

Clearance

The chair cannot assume that because a vacancy is imminent it can be filled immediately. The dean of a school or college is usually the person who must decide whether a vacant position can be filled. When the dean must turn back unspent salary dollars, which would mean that even a temporary replacement could not be approved, the departmental faculty will have to double up on courses or drop some from the regular schedule. If the dean does not need the unused salary that results when a faculty member leaves in the middle of an academic term, then the authorization to find a temporary replacement may be given immediately.

At institutions with strong centralized budgetary control of positions, the chief academic officer may have to approve use of unspent salary funds and approve any requests to fill a vacant position. The institutional budget officer may also have to approve the request by confirming that the vacant position is a regularly authorized position supported by general funds. Thus, the chair's dean, the dean of faculties or vice president for academic affairs, and the institution's budget officer might all have to agree to filling a vacant position. Similarly, they would need to approve the budget for a *new* position and an identification number or budget line number for the position.

Restructuring the Position

A dean of faculty or equivalent officer may require that an existing vacant position be assigned a new rank, salary, or other characteristics. Administrative officials may wish to enhance some new academic specialty or area of research, requiring a different set of disciplinary skills. New interdepartmental responsibilities may be built into the position. Seldom are the same old functions and responsibilities duplicated, providing the chair has a unique opportunity to shape the position. Financial constraints may play a role in restructuring a position; they need to be identified as early as possible. The chair should, at this stage, conceptualize the position in relation to the departmental plan (Poort 1971).

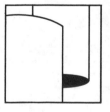

Determination of Salary

Salary is of great importance in recruiting faculty, mainly because faculty salaries have not kept pace with inflation and consequently have fallen behind salary levels for comparable professions and business (Heim 1980, p. 15). This matter assumes substantial importance when a department attempts to recruit for an associate or full professorship.

Three sets of issues are related to determining salary during this preliminary planning period. First is the matter of salary equity for women. Second is the decision to hire part-time (rather than full-time) faculty and the method of paying them. Third is the level of salary and the rank to be assigned a full-time position.

The issue of equitable pay for women (and minorities) is a long-standing one (Bayer and Astin 1975; Bunzel 1982; Greenhouse 1981, 1982; Prather 1971; Sandler 1979). The most frequently given reasons (allegedly unrelated to discrimination) for the difference among, for example, academic scientists are as follows:

- As a class, women tend to face a greater constraint on career mobility if married (especially those in nonprofessional jobs).
- Women are more likely to interrupt their careers for child bearing and rearing, thereby losing years of experience.
- They entered the better-paying scientific disciplines in smaller proportions, thereby keeping the average salary down for women scientists.
- They have acquired their degrees in large numbers only recently, so that the younger and hence lower paid professionals dominate this subgroup of scientists (Lawrence 1981, p. 334).

The facts may not fit this stereotype, however. Lawrence's article reports on a study (Ahern and Scott) that examined how well matched samples of men and women Ph.D. scientists fared, relative to each other, in climbing the pay scale and academic ladder. The findings from the statistical analysis reveal, using the same "explanatory" items stated previously, that:

- Women scientists are at least as mobile as men, regardless of whether they marry or have children.
- Fewer than half of all women with Ph.D.s have children, and of them, only 10 percent with small children drop out of the labor force.
- Even when women were matched to men by scientific subfield, by years of experience, by years since graduation, and by prestige of the department in which they were

employed, their average salaries lagged behind those of men. For example, among those who earned their Ph.D.s after 1975—the group where differentials proved smallest—women's academic salaries trailed men's from $400 (2 percent) in mathematics to $2,100 (10 percent) in the biological sciences to $3,300 (15 percent) in chemistry (Lawrence 1981, p. 331).

The authors of the study concluded that de facto salary discrimination against women is a more appropriate explanation for the differences in pay. The message to department chairs is that they should examine the salary ranges and levels to be paid new faculty in comparison to what others are receiving in the same institution for the approximate same workload. If the salary authorized by the dean or administrative officials does not meet this test, then the chair should formally notify the dean of the potential problems with grievances and sex discrimination lawsuits.

Financial stringencies are making it more difficult for institutions to authorize replacements, regardless of the course-enrollment load on a department. Some institutions may use attrition to reduce the size of the faculty as costs rise and enrollments level off or decline. Others may even allow enrollments to increase because they need the tuition revenue. In such instances, a department usually has only two options: increase the size of classes or convince the dean to permit the department to hire part-time faculty. The latter practice has become so widespread that most community colleges now employ more part-time than full-time faculty. The largest benefit of this practice, which grows with each term, is the apparent cost savings (President's Council 1980; Russell 1980). The institution need not pay matching retirement shares or contributions toward health, life, or accident insurance. Only teaching duties have to be paid for, making it possible to relate direct instructional costs (salaries, etc.) to tuition received, revenue received from state appropriations per student, or other source of income. Under these considerations, part-time faculty should be paid some flat fee per credit hour, with a fractional supplement should a class exceed a given size, say 35 students.

Several different factors need to be considered in the determination of salary for full-time faculty. A first consideration relates to the amount of money available if the position was filled by a person who received a high salary. The chair should consider subdividing the salary by creating at least one *new* position, thereby making two vacancies available. (This action may be the only way to create new positions in the future.)

Normally, a replacement will be brought in at the entry level salary for an assistant professor. If the ABD (the doctoral candidate who has completed *all but dissertation*) is to be accepted, a lesser salary and rank may be offered, with the promise of an increase when the advanced degree is received. Because some ABD's are almost at the point of defending their dissertation, they may be brought in at some intermediate salary. Because salary rates are most often the dean's responsibility, the chair may succeed in obtaining a better salary base by preparing a case that includes all the variables that traditionally impact salary levels—market competition, alternative employment, in and out of higher education, reputation of the discipline, the candidate's record of productivity and prospects, equal employment opportunity and affirmative action, accreditation of the program by professional associations and state agencies, program priorities for the college and department, commitments to improve quality.

In attempting to set an appropriate salary, the chair and the dean should consider the possibility of the candidate's supplemental income, perhaps from summer teaching (most common), teaching elsewhere, consulting, private practice, royalties, lecture fees, or research salaries (Heim 1980, p. 15). In some locations, faculty are much more likely to find such opportunities for supplemental income. While it may be tempting to set a lower salary because faculty could avail themselves of these supplemental opportunities, the chair and the dean should consider the possible detrimental effects on the quality of performance on the full-time job. In the long run, it may cost less to establish a higher salary.

Guidelines for an Affirmative Action Search

With preliminary approval to fill a vacancy, it is next necessary to obtain a copy of the institution's latest guidelines for affirmative action or, at the least, a written set of procedures to be followed—*before* the position description is rewritten or advertising is developed. Completing a case file to demonstrate the fairness of recruitment is much easier when the requirements are known at the beginning of the search. A department needs an affirmative action component in its recruitment policy or, at

Completing a case file to demonstrate the fairness of recruitment is much easier when the requirements are known at the beginning of the search.

a minimum, a written set of procedures to be followed. Some typical items to be included might be:

- Who (the position title) is to appoint a search and screening committee, if one is to be used
- The size and composition of such committee, whether it is to have student members, and how the chair will be selected
- Any alternative screening procedures to be used in place of a committee and who would be responsible to see that any search is carried out properly and on time
- The administrator or staff person responsible for keeping applicants' documents and files and a statement about removing pictures and any other inappropriate information on the application
- The arrangements for obtaining and recording information on race and sex of candidates and nominees
- The person—for example, the president—who can give final approval for a job offer, which gives the candidate some legal recourse should the appointment not materialize because of institutional rather than departmental difficulties.

A substantial commitment by a department to implement a change in the racial and sexual composition of its faculty would involve the following:

- Establishment of realistic goals (in a written plan or policy statement) for the share of faculty it desires to be identified as minority or female members
- Projections of when these goals might be achieved, given the faculties' departure rates, availability of vacancies, availability of candidates, etc., by year
- Establishment of a set of procedures that when followed would represent a serious effort to locate and recruit qualified minorities and women
- A procedure of reviewing the original plan, monitoring its implementation, and revising its goals as necessary.

A written statement of action about each goal would constitute a departmental plan for affirmative action if the college or university has none or a department wants to make explicit its commitment to fair employment.

After goals, interim projections, and timetables have been established, the procedures for recruiting minorities need to be specified. The following list indicates the kinds of contacts and those who should be notified so that information about a vacancy has a chance of reaching potential minority or woman candidates:

1. Solicited suggestions from minority members and women on the institution's faculty
2. Letters, telephone calls, interviews, and personal meetings with members of professional and scholarly organizations and associations
3. Paid advertising in newspapers and professional publications
4. Notices to private placement services specializing in referral of minority and women candidates
5. Notices to appropriate college and university (graduate) placement offices, including historically black or female institutions
6. Notices to public placement or employment services
7. Contacts of all kinds with discipline departments and professional schools in appropriate colleges and universities, including historically black or female institutions
8. Notices to business, industry, and governmental agencies related to academic areas and specialties
9. Notices to such organizations as the Urban League, Community Action Agency, NOW
10. Public news stories outlining the institution's commitment to equal opportunity employment practices

The need for and desired character of genuine affirmative action plans in higher education can be found in *The Case for Affirmative Action for Blacks in Higher Education* (Fleming, Gill, and Swinton 1978). It also provides a history of federal affirmative action programs and the constitutional authority supporting them (pp. 48–77). A special report by the Carnegie Council on Policy Studies in Higher Education (1975) also delineates the character of desired affirmative action plans. These and other studies find that the decentralized decision-making system of many colleges and universities often poses a challenge to the institutions with reasonably well-organized equal employment programs.

Summary

Before any effort to recruit replacements begins, a chair must be authorized to fill the vacancy. The important characteristics desired in the new faculty member need to be conceptualized, based on the rate of enrollments and the institution's needs during the past 2 or 3 years. An appropriate salary and rank must be determined. A fair recruiting process begins by reviewing the institution's guidelines for affirmative action. No longer is it acceptable for an institution to say it has been unable to find any qualified minorities or women unless a thorough search was planned and carried out. Chairs need to understand what kinds of action plans are considered realistic and authentic.

The department head usually has the central responsibility for carrying out the recruiting process. Nevertheless, it is important to involve the faculty at the earliest stage and to ask a faculty member to chair the search committee before the vacancy is announced and advertised.

The Search Committee

The search committee should be chaired by a faculty member; its members should include other departmental faculty, a faculty person from outside the department, and possibly one or more students from the class levels the new instructor would likely teach. The department chair must make it clear that this committee will have a key role in reviewing all candidates' applications and credentials but that the committee's recommendations are almost always advisory to the chair (Sommerfield and Nagely 1974; Strohm 1974).

One of the search committee's first tasks is to review a description of the position (Wolotkiewicz 1980, p. 68). The department chair must ensure that the description is current and accurate and that departmental faculty understand it. If additional information needs to be added to the description, the department head and search committee chair should draft a new statement. It is particularly important to identify the areas of expertise desired of applicants. The courses to be taught and other activities for which the person will be responsible (such as "freshman advisor") should be identified. It may be necessary to specify the number of students for which the person will be advisor. The research skills needed for the position should be mentioned, but if the minimum degree required is less than a doctorate, it probably is not necessary to list or mention research skills *unless* an ABD candidate would be acceptable.

The departmental faculty must see the job description and have time to react to it. Some current faculty members might be willing to develop a new specialty to enhance his own career so that the new person could be assigned to teach an existing set of courses.

Preparing an Announcement of the Vacancy

Announcements of the vacancy should be prepared in a short version and a long version. The short one should be specifically designed for use as an advertisement. The long one, containing a thorough description of the position, its good and weak points, the conditions of employment, and the specific expectations for the next occupant of the position, can be used in direct mail solicitation sent to equivalent departments in other institutions and to members of appropriate professional associations. It also should be sent to all candidates who have indicated on interest in the position, so that all will be equally informed about the position.

At the very least, the following items* should be contained in the short advertisement:

- *Closing date for applications*: This date may be left open, but the position should be readvertised for at least a week when a definite closing date is determined.

- (1) *Rank or ranks assignable* may be "open," depending upon experience; (2) *position number in budget*: A unique identification number in the budget for the position should be listed, particularly when two or more positions are advertised; (3) *degree(s) required*: State whether an ABD is acceptable or whether candidates should have a master's degree, a doctorate, or a master's degree plus 5 years academic experience. Describe areas from which the terminal degree should come.

- *Department name, with degree programs offered*: Give the full name of the department and identify the predominant discipline if it is not revealed in the name. List degrees offered, e.g., B.S., M.S., Ph.D., or Ed.D.

- *Salary or salary range*: Include the regular period of appointment, e.g., $14,000–$16,000 for 10 months. If supplemental salary is possible through summer appointments, overload work, or something similar, it can be listed, but it should be accompanied by a realistic qualifying statement.

- *Period of employment*: Give the exact period of employment (combined with the previous statement and the following statement as necessary).

- *Conditions of contract*: Explain clearly whether the contract is renewable and whether tenure can be earned, and any special requirements.

*Several of these items were adapted from affirmative action materials prepared over several years by officials at Florida State University (1980).

- *Special characteristics or expertise desired*: Include the field of specialization, subspecialties within a discipline, any special responsibilities or characteristics (research skills, experience in program development, service work, for example, or previous experience of any kind).
- *Full mailing address and telephone number(s) of person who can answer questions about the position and the search*: If the institution is not well known or is located in a rural area, it will help to explain the location. For example, in parentheses below the mailing address add "30 miles north of _____ " or "50 miles south of _____ ."

The advertisement should also include the following items if they are applicable:

- "An affirmative action, equal opportunity employer." While it is not absolutely necessary that this statement or one like it be included in the advertisement, a college or university that is trying to observe those principles should include it (Knowles 1970, II, pp. 6–32). An announcement should indicate whether a college is church sponsored and hires only members of its faith.
- Planned informal or formal interviews at a professional conference or in some adjacent metropolitan area should be mentioned, giving the specific dates and places.
- If the position is in music or the arts, specific instructions should be included about the need to send tape recordings or a portfolio (Ross 1981).

It is not necessary to give complete details about the position, the department, the college, or the university in the short announcement, but such information should be available and sent to all applicants who inquire. Brochures about the institution, its separate units and special programs, and any other information about the department can be combined in a package with the long announcement to be sent to all who inquire. It is not necessary to include a college catalog in this package.

The long announcement should repeat the information in the advertisement but with some important details added. The most important part of the announcement should be the instructions about submitting credentials. Some additional items in the long announcement would include:

- *Letters of reference*: Usually three letters are sufficient. They should have been written within the past 6 months or so. A search committee's or an institution's request for letters written about the candidate's suitability for a *particular* position must be clearly stated (Lewis 1971). If a committee or institution will not be able to use the references in a placement file but the file is desired anyway, that should be explained. If the committee wants full mailing addresses and telephone numbers for all references, the announcement should clearly say so.
- *Current resume or curriculum vita*: The committee should specify that it wants detailed information about a person's education, related activities, honors, assistantships, scholarships, research, publications, grants and contracts, work in progress, and so on.

- *Letter of application*: The committee may want the applicant to indicate the earliest reasonable date he could be available to begin work, the approximate salary below which the candidate would not accept a job offer, and any other requirements that if unmet would prevent the candidate from accepting a position.
- *Copies of any recent publications.*
- *The minimum materials required for the application file*: At a prominent place in the long announcement, include a statement defining the minimum information necessary about an applicant *before* his or her file will be evaluated.

A number of items should *not* be requested at any time during the entire recruiting process: race, national origin, sex, age, handicap, family plans, maiden name, and any other information precluded under guidelines for affirmative action and equal employment opportunity. (The name a candidate may have used during previous employment may be requested to determine if it was different from the current one.)

The committee needs to make it clear that it will not consider incomplete applications. It also must announce whether it will consider applications that are incomplete at the closing date but complete by the time the committee meets for the first time to review applicants' credentials. A grace period would ensure receipt of the applications postmarked on the closing day.

The institution's affirmative action officer should be sent copies of the short advertisement and the long announcement.

In some institutions, the officer must approve the copy *before* it is sent out. The function of this official is to ensure that the institution carries out a fair recruitment program; he may have prepared a check list to guide the search process so that it will conform to national and state policy.

Announcing the Vacancy

The search committee chair and the departmental support staff should compile a mailing list of institutions and people who can identify qualified candidates for the vacancy. Information about the geographic origins of faculty and staff is of prime importance in compiling a mailing list of places to send announcements of a vacancy. Many colleges and universities serve a regional population and draw people to its faculty who are residents of the region (Mitchell and Starr 1971). A regional profile of a department's faculty—i.e., the states, areas, and counties faculty come from, the high schools they graduated from, the places they call "home," the locations of their undergraduate colleges and graduate schools—tends to define the manpower supply area. This information is important when an institution needs to explain its national or regional character or has other special characteristics that it can claim have largely determined the sexual and racial composition of its faculty (Smelser and Content 1980). More importantly, any demonstration of affirmative action should show the institution reaching beyond the traditional supply areas.

State departments of education, state coordinating agencies for postsecondary education, statewide equal employment job agencies, and statewide associations for private institutions are good sources of statewide job registers. Circulating announcements to these sources helps ensure their reaching a diversified population, increasing the department's participation in affirmative action.

State and regional associations of the department's discipline may compile a list of job openings. If they do not, their membership lists would provide a source of potential candidates. Departments in other institutions with graduate programs in the discipline are another source of potential candidates.

Large regional, comprehensive institutions need to advertise in nationwide publications for at least a month. They are usually published by the disciplinary and professional associations, but others that might be included are *Academe* and *Science*.

The Chronicle of Higher Education is appropriate for many kinds of positions (Marcus 1977), but the more specialized the position the greater the need to work with a national association. Almost all of the national disciplinary associations have special committees to facilitate placement of minorities and women.

Another approach is to identify traditional women's and black's colleges and universities with graduate programs. The results of a nationwide survey of blacks in higher education revealed that 80 percent of the 1,054 respondents "heard about job vacancies from other blacks and nontraditional search procedures" (Moore and Wagstaff 1974, p. 43). Thus, both current black faculty members and the institutions they recommend should be canvassed. Seeking candidates, especially blacks, requires the kind of effort a football or basketball coach undertakes.

Serious consideration of requirements for affirmative action in advertising positions often raises questions about which positions and personnel changes have to be advertised. This check list developed in Florida for items not required to be advertised seems to work reasonably well.

Seeking candidates, especially blacks, requires the kind of effort a football or basketball coach undertakes.

- Promotion from assistant to associate professor
- Chair or assistant chair, when the existing faculty rotate through the chair. Recruiting for an external chair should be advertised in the normal way, however
- A principal investigator or recipient of a contract or grant
- Change of a funding source for an existing position, as from a grant or contract to a regularly funded general budget, provided that duties are not significantly changed as a result of the shift in funding
- Visiting scholars or exchange professorships
- Positions less than half-time during a term
- "Adjunct" or visiting or other temporary faculty who are not appointed for more than a year (Florida State University 1980).

To be *included* under the guidelines for affirmative action are all instructional and research positions for half-time or more.

If the rank, salary, or some other important aspect of the position is changed after advertising begins or is completed, the changed position should be readvertised at least 2 more weeks.

Keeping Records

The records of the entire search and screening process must be kept systematically and well secured in places known to the head secretary, the department chair, and the search committee chair. They should be kept in a central location. A record of all mailings should include the dates mailed and a list of recipients, particularly women and minorities. Whenever a new application is received, it should be dated and a file created for that person. All first-time applicants or inquirers should be sent a copy of the long announcement, which could be accompanied by a statement about the affirmative action program explaining that people found eligible who remain in active consideration for the position will be sent a survey form asking for certain information about race, sex, and other data that will be used in the aggregate to document the characteristics of qualified applicants. (The chair should arrange with the affirmative action official to have these surveys returned to the affirmative action office.)

A check list of materials received should be placed in each applicant's file to quickly determine whether the file is complete. The application files should be grouped alphabetically by last name. The first task on the day after the application period closes is to compile a list of all people who have inquired about the vacancy and to place an "x" by the name of all people whose files are *in*complete. If all documents arrive before the first meeting of the search committee, the "x" should be removed. One of the search committee's first tasks is to confirm the incomplete files and retire those files from further consideration.

The remaining files should all have a letter, memo, or personal note of application, a current resume or vita or placement file, three or more letters of reference or three reference statements in the current placement file, examples of any written work, and any other items required. To be fair, no pictures should be included in the files; they should be removed by the person opening the mail, correctly identified, and kept in a separate file. If an applicant submits too much extraneous material, it should be filed along with the pictures. All records should be kept for at least 3 years for each recruitment effort.

SCREENING APPLICANTS' FILES

Screening of applicants' files begins with a determination of who is eligible from among all the candidates, first by excluding those who do not meet the criteria published in the institution's policy guidelines and second by excluding those who do not meet the requirements for the position stated in the advertisements or announcements. During these first screenings, it is important to make explicit those candidates who have received some preferential attention. Those candidates who lack only a few details of a requirement should be left in the eligible group for evaluation at the next stage.

The group of eligible applicants become the nominees for the position. Reviewing the files to decide who is best qualified for the position is done in two steps: selecting the top 10 to 12 nominees, then reducing the list to the best three to five people. Extensive efforts to check references and credentials may be necessary before the final set of nominees recommended for a campus visit become the official candidates for the position.

Ineligible Applicants

The search committee needs to define the criteria for determining which applicants will be declared ineligible as well as how it will proceed when it feels equity and fairness would be served if it violated its own policies. Only rarely does a set of policies cover all contingencies. A search committee could establish that any of its procedures may be altered temporarily by a unanimous (or three-quarters) vote and submission of a written resolution explaining the perceived need.

The committee might first declare ineligible those whose files are incomplete at the time of the committee's first meeting and those whose files are postmarked after the closing date. It is important to agree that hand-delivered applications be received before the closing date expires; normally no travel grace period should be permitted for hand-delivered applications.

A second group of applicants to be declared ineligible could be those who are relatives or dependents of the department chair or dean (Cosper 1970). The restriction against nepotism can be applied broadly without exceptions or it can be defined narrowly, permitting relatives to be employed as long as they are not under the direct supervision of a relative already employed (Pinegree et al. 1978). (See Moore and Wagstaff 1974, p. 156, for a comment on this practice and the employment of black women in black colleges.)

The committee should decide whether it wants to include doctoral candidates finishing a dissertation as eligible nominees. In the past, when there was a shortage of Ph.D.s, it was common to accept ABDs as bona fide applicants, but with no current shortage, the committee may decide it wants to accept only full Ph.D.s.

A fourth class of applicants who might be excluded is the game-players— those who state in the letter that they will complete the file if the institution is seriously interested. If the applicants were sent the long announcement, it should be assumed that they can read and that failure to complete an application is part of their game, designed to benefit themselves and not the search committee. If the committee chair says the committee is truly interested, then that may create false expectations as well as questions about fairness to the other applicants with incomplete files. When one or two applicants have incomplete files and appear to be highly qualified, it may seem beneficial to solicit the missing documents, but fairness would dictate that a follow-up letter be sent to every applicant with an incomplete file.

Another class of applicants that the committee may choose to declare ineligible are alumni of the department or the institution (Miller 1977), although professional schools may recruit people with skills developed by discipline departments in another college of the same university. Herman B. Wells, the president who built Indiana University in Bloomington, suggested that it would be beneficial to have a faculty 30 to 40 percent of whose members were alumni of IU. The benefit of such a percentage would be in an excellent faculty who understood the traditions of the institution and who would help keep them alive, in turn helping other alumni to continue to identify with the university and provide political and financial support when needed. The best opportunity to implement that policy, however, would come after a doctoral graduate had made a name for himself at another institution and then returned to the alma mater. Doing so would remove the possible suspicion that he would be under the influence of a former professor or other faculty committee members and would prevent his being perceived as a permanent junior colleague. If alumni do apply for the vacancy, the committee should begin informal inquiries about officials' receptivity to the idea. It may be that local graduates can be hired by submitting a detailed letter of justification, but if the institution already employs a large number of its own graduates, administrators may feel it is time to look elsewhere for new blood. The important factor to keep in balance is to ensure that this form of academic inbreeding does not stifle the recruitment of diverse viewpoints.

The chair of the search committee has the task of identifying clearly ineligible and questionable applicants. At its first meeting, the search committee should decide which questionable applications should be cut and note the basis for the decisions on the check sheet in each affected applicant's file. These files should be removed from the active group.

Applicants from Preferential Recruitment

Applicants resulting from a preferential recruitment most often are people familiar to search committee members, other departmental faculty, or institutional officials (Caplow and McGee 1958). Applicants who are known may be given special consideration because they are thought to be people who will be much less likely to produce undesirable surprises after they are appointed. While its value in avoiding social misfits is apparent, such a practice is unfortunately highly restrictive and encourages avoidance of unknown but talented people, particularly women and minorities. The definition of "undesirable" tends to be highly subjective.

The vestiges of this practice are still evident, but the mode of operation is somewhat different (Marcus 1977; Roper 1980). Copies of the long announcement might be sent to professional acquaintances several weeks before the short advertisement is published. Faculty might telephone colleagues and friends to ask whether they know of anyone who would qualify for the job. While they have been quite successful, the existence of these "old boy networks" has led to the creation of similar "old girl networks," with the added twist that they can help women identify sexist departments and institutions to avoid them or challenge them.

The search committee needs to consider the use of preferential recruitment and decide how to use the system's strengths and neutralize its weaknesses (Smelser and Content 1980). "Full disclosure" is one such practice; for example, search committee members and other faculty can reveal (1) which applicants they know personally and (2) the ones to which they would give better than average consideration because they were recommended by trusted colleagues. These applicants might be coded "P1" and "P2" to indicate their respective relationship

The existence of these "old boy networks" has led to the creation of similar "old girl networks," with the added twist that they can help women identify sexist departments and institutions to avoid them or challenge them.

to search committee members. The search committee might want to decide that these applicants would have to have records and credentials that would make them obviously better than nonpreferential applicants. An applicant who is known personally by a faculty member should not be coded preferential if the application is unsubstantiated by a written record and outside references. If a candidate is labeled preferential because of some special characteristic, then the nonpreferential applicants should be given an equal chance to submit evidence about their possessing the desirable characteristic. The committee should send a letter requesting such information to *all* candidates. All applicants should have the opportunity to submit the additional information, or the information should be excluded from consideration.

Determining Eligible Applicants

The second cut of the original applicants should result from comparing each applicant's credentials with the *advertised* requirements. The search committee must agree upon the characteristics of the position *before* it is advertised, and each member must have a copy of the advertisement and the announcement when evaluating the files. The committee's formal agreement to use the advertised characteristics as criteria must be taken seriously and strictly adhered to unless unusual circumstances intervene. As many as one-half of the applicants may have submitted all credentials but not provided evidence that they possess the specific characteristics required, hoping they might be seriously considered if someone closely examines the record of their experience and achievements. The evaluation of the credentials should be recorded on each applicant's check sheet. Separate lines should be provided on the check sheet for each of the position's major requirements. A space for comments could be used to note such things as "inappropriate specialization," "wrong degree," "insufficient experience," etc.

If every applicant is sent a long announcement, it too may be used to evaluate applicants' files. For this reason, the additional mandatory requirements for a complete application must be stated very clearly in the long announcement. The check sheet for each file should contain separate lines for these additional items, and appropriate comments should be entered about deficiencies.

The search committee should consider retaining "marginal" applicants, the people who are almost qualified. Some may never have submitted an application previously and may not have prepared it well. It would be appropriate to code these files ''M'' during the review for the first cut to ensure that they are given another full reading at the next screening. If the marginal applicants do not survive the next review, which should be the first one based on a positive judgment of candidates, then their application files should be retired.

The entire search committee should consider the files of all applicants whom the chair recommends to be cut because they have not met the criteria in the advertisement and the announcement. Each committee member should then be assigned to review a portion of the remaining files of those tentatively judged as qualified to verify if, in fact, all of them meet the advertised criteria. If any additional unqualified applicants are found, the entire committee should review their files. Differing interpretations should be worked out amicably, but a secret ballot may be needed to resolve a sticky case. These cases might be designated as marginal applicants, which would automatically move them to the next state of consideration.

Those applicants who do not survive the second cut should be noted on the master list of applicants and their files pulled from further consideration. The remaining applicants now become the official pool of *nominees* for the available position.

Evaluating Nominees' Files

The surviving group of nominees will now have been judged to meet the minimum set of requirements for the position. In this next step, the evaluation should focus on the characteristics of the nominees to determine the best qualified among them.

Each search committee member will now need to read each applicant's file and select the top six to ten nominees. The chair should compile committee member's lists into an aggregate list. That list then becomes the focus of the committee's third meeting, at which each committee member explains his choices and enumerates the candidates' strengths and weaknesses. The chair next attempts to develop a consensus about the rank order of nominees. The objective of this meeting is to select the top three to five nominees, any of whom would be clearly acceptable to the faculty.

The top nominees might include one or more of the marginal applicants. Furthermore, some of the top nominees might be much stronger on a secondary characteristic than on a primary one. For example, a person who is expert and well published in research but without formal teaching experience or without teaching experience in the subject area needed may have a significant ranking, but if teaching is the primary function of the position, the committee should decide who is more appropriate for the available position. Selecting a researcher when a teacher is needed may result in the position's being vacant again before long.

The really difficult situation for a search committee arises when almost none of the top five to six nominees are very impressive. In the uncertain 1980s, many well-qualified faculty may prefer to remain where they are than to risk making a horizontal career move. They may prefer remaining in a relatively unsatisfactory position in the middle of a seniority list than moving to a somewhat more desirable career position but at the bottom of someone else's seniority roster.

In this difficult situation, the committee can recommend that the most promising of an average group be invited for a campus interview, or it can advise the department chair to reopen the search. Before choosing the latter, the search committee must correctly assess the image of the department that is being communicated to outsiders and answer some questions: Do the nominees seem to fit the "real" image of the department? If some nominees are desired who would more closely fit the *desired* image of the department, would more salary have to be offered? additional rank? tenure? little or no teaching assignment? Can the department afford any of these added inducements? If the answer to that question is "yes," then the search committee should recommend a change in the characteristics desired for the position and a new start for the search. If the answer is "no," then it may be best to proceed with arrangements for the campus visits for the best qualified nominees.

The search committee with an acceptable group of nominees should rank them in order. If only one or two are clearly consensus nominees, then the committee should forward only one or two names to the department chair. It should resist submitting a predetermined number of names if fewer candidates are desirable. The chair of the search committee should draft a memorandum to the department chair stating the strengths and weaknesses of the nominees.

The department chair, having received the committee's recommendations and the appropriate files, faces a major decision before inviting the nominees to campus—whether to check more than two or three references for each nominee. If there is some question about a nominee, then all references would be checked before the invitation is issued to the nominee. What should one search for in checking references? Initially, level of competence, promise of career growth, ability to work with colleagues and students, outstanding achievements and other strengths, and certain weaknesses—missing classes, not completing work on time, complaints by students.

One difficulty facing a chair is how to check references of a nominee who does not want his current employer to know he is contemplating a move. In that case, the chair should telephone the nominee and explain that he is a nominee but cannot be considered for a campus interview until references are checked. If the nominee cannot suggest some other references, then he must be dropped. Similarly, if a nominee has submitted only a placement file or letters of reference that are older than 2 years, then he should be asked to arrange immediately for current reference letters to be sent.

If the letters of reference are unspecific and do not evaluate the nominee factually or very positively, then all the nominee's references should be checked (Nelson 1981). If references show a lack of unqualified support for the nominee or if the nominee is described as nearly perfect, than it is appropriate to ask the original references for two other people who would know the nominee, call this second group, and ask for a third list. This network of 10 to 15 references is usually sufficient to clear up uncertainties but more might be necessary. The chair must determine whether a negative comment is an isolated report or general agreement about a person and whether glowing reports are merely part of the respondent's style.

One of the nagging fears of a search committee, department chairperson, college dean and the dean of faculties is that a genuinely undesirable person will be hired. The kinds of personal conduct which cause the most problems and should be listened for in these interviews are: pernicious irascibility, mental health problems, alcoholism, criminal behavior, dismissal from a college or university in the last five years, and disciplinary action in the last two or three years. Persons found to be described with any of these problems need some absolutely sterling qualities to remain under serious consideration.

The search committee chair may be asked to contact the references and to prepare a written summary of the information learned. The department chair will have to decide how desirable or undesirable each nominee is. A nominee might have to be dropped from consideration as a result of the reference checks. If minor discrepancies are found on important characteristics, they should be clarified with the nominee, over the phone or during the campus visit.

As soon as all the nominees have been checked, the support staff should send each a package of materials before they visit the campus—a faculty handbook, an institutional catalog, a copy of the collective bargaining agreement if one exists, an overview of the state system (if one exists, for public institutions), and any separate statements about a continuing contract or tenure status, opportunities for career advancement, academic freedom, grievance procedures, the annual contract, the annual budget, notice required for personnel actions, fringe benefits, and patent and copyright policy (Miner 1973). Many of the latter items are contained in the faculty handbook or faculty bargaining agreement.

THE CAMPUS VISIT AND FINAL DECISIONS

The campus visit, which can be used to persuade a candidate to accept a job offer, is arranged after almost all questions about a nominee have been answered satisfactorily. Like the first of the process, the dean's approval must be sought before bringing candidates to campus or making a job offer. It is always possible that none of the candidates will accept an offer, making it necessary to decide whether to reopen the search.

Reviewing the Search Committee's Recommendations

Once the search committee has completed its work and its chair has written recommendations to the department head, the next step is to complete arrangements for the candidates to visit the campus. It is now appropriate to check the authenticity of the credentials, which becomes doubly important if it was not possible to check very many of the personal references. The purpose of this effort is to verify the facts about the candidate on his credentials and his veracity and to obtain confirming information about the candidate's perceived strengths. Candidates may be found to have lied about their education, degrees, salary records, arrest records, and reasons for leaving past jobs (Butterfield 1981; Nelson 1981).

The following list of important actions should be undertaken before any candidates are invited for a campus visit:

- Check academic qualifications by calling the registrar of the awarding institutions.
- Reread the resume to find unclear or incomplete information. Phone the candidate to ask about any gaps in employment or long periods between degrees.
- Make sure the candidate has signed some kind of statement that all information contained in the resume is true and correct to the best of his knowledge, and make sure that the candidate knows that a person can be terminated for lying on the official application.
- Conduct a telephone network check of the candidate's references if it has not already been done to learn enough not to be surprised during the campus interview, to develop questions to be asked during the interview, and to learn additional information about the candidates.

With a fairly clear picture of each candidate's strengths and weaknesses, the department head needs to review the candidates' qualifications in relations to the department's goals. Often the strongest candidate may be seen by the chair as the one with the best research record, even when the department supports little research. If the goal of the department is to change its image and improve its record of research productivity, then this goal should have been incorporated in the position description. In essence, the search committee should be told in advance if it is to select the candidate with the best research or publication record. The department head has four choices after receiving a list of candidates and verifying their credentials: (1) arrange with the dean to obtain funds to bring the candidates to campus; (2) select only two of the candidates and arrange with the dean to bring them to campus; (3) send the list back to the search committee with additional instructions, risking noncooperation or low morale; (4) begin arrangements to readvertise the position, after changing certain criteria and information. The last choice may be the most appropriate if one or more applicant's files came in after the closing date and few acceptable applicants were found among the original group.

Conferring with the Dean

The dean or his representative should be given a preview of the candidates, perhaps when requesting travel funds for them to visit campus. If the department head has not kept the dean informed about the selection process, snags can easily develop at this point. This is not the time to find out that the position should be filled only with a woman or minority person, or with a young person to bring in new ideas, or with an out-of-state person. It is not the time to discover that no tenure time will be credited for a new assistant professor or that the money could also be used to give raises to current faculty. While some of these stipulations patently violate affirmative action policy and guidelines, they are not uncommon. But, most importantly, *most of these problems can be worked out before this meeting with the dean.*

Telephoning the Candidates

With approval from the dean, the chair can now telephone each candidate and invite him or her to campus on some mutually acceptable date. (Each visit should be scheduled so that there is at least one day between candidate's visits.) The first item to be discussed during the call is whether the candidate is still interested in the position. The chair must ascertain that the candidate understands the pay range, the rank, and other vital information about the position. This is also the time to clarify other items that the search committee has raised and that emerged while checking references. If everything is satisfactory, the chair invites each candidate to prepare a formal presentation (Sawyer 1974) and to be ready to talk about his or her work and plans. The chair should confirm details of the phone conversation by letter.

The Campus Visit

The primary purpose of the campus visit should be to persuade the candidate to accept a job offer (McKeachie 1972, p. 45). It is extremely important to make each candidate feel that he or she is welcome and will be accepted by the faculty and students. Consequently, someone should pick up the candidates at the airport, take them to their lodging, and escort them across campus and to appointments. A cold reception, a crowded schedule, and missed appointments communicate to a candidate that none of the local faculty are taking the visit seriously.

Each candidate should be asked to prepare a formal lecture or paper and deliver it to an audience of students and faculty. Each candidate will be interviewed by the department head, the search committee as a group, various groups of faculty, a group of student leaders, someone from the dean's office, and a central administrative official. The interviews should be conducted with civility and friendliness. Questions that are off limits are those related to marital status, family plans, and other sex-specific topics not directly related to the professional character of the position.

The search committee chair should see that each person who will be interviewing and/or listening to the public lecture of each candidate receives a simple evaluation form. It should contain four to six characteristics that are to be evaluated and rated and space to enter comments about the characteristics. The forms should be returned to the chair within 1 week of the candidate's visit, preferably on the same day as the observations were made. The search committee chair should compile the rating data in a standard format so that the candidates can be compared fairly.

The Committee's Final Evaluation

The chair of the search committee and the department head should call a meeting of the search committee as soon as possible after all candidates have visited the campus. They should

---

review each candidate's ratings, clarify points of difference, discuss each candidate's strengths and weaknesses, and decide on the best one or two (Lewin and Duchan 1971). The committee should agree on the best first and second choices and make its recommendation to the department head.

The Dean's Choice
Often the dean will not want to receive the final list of desired candidates in rank order, merely a simple alphabetical list in the official memorandum accompanied by credentials and references sent from the department. The dean may have some further questions that the department head should be prepared to answer:

- Is any of the candidates a woman or a member of a minority group?
- Does the candidate look better on paper than in person? If so, what personal characteristics seem to hurt this person as a candidate?
- What was the candidate's energy image? Active? Normal? Lethargic?
- What was communicated by the candidate's body stance? Nervous? Relaxed? Unsure? Confused? Defensive? Rigid?
- What was seen in his facial expressions? Openness? Sneering? Puzzlement? Pleasantness? Boredom? Interest?
- Were the expected weaknesses of the candidate confirmed by the visit? Were other weaknesses identified? Were strengths confirmed? New ones revealed? Did he or she show genuine promise?
- Has the candidate misrepresented himself? Positively? Negatively? Are there any problems?

The Job Offer
When the dean approves a job offer and indicates his preference among the candidates, the department head telephones the prime candidate to confirm the acceptable salary, the position's rank, and the time when the candidate can be placed on the institution's payroll.* The candidate may want some time to consider the final offer; a week or two should be sufficient

---

*Affirmative action procedures would be violated if a position were filled or a firm job offer made *before* the application date expires.

(Seyfried et al. 1977) If the candidate opens the telephone call with a request for time to consider the offer, the chair needs to decide whether to raise the salary offer or to add some other perquisite to convince the candidate to accept the offer. A candidate with some time to make a decision may want to seek a counteroffer from his present employer, and the chair should understand what is happening. It might be helpful to grant the chair the authority to offer a short-term consulting contract to the candidate for preparing a new curriculum program proposal or for compiling data and preparing a funding proposal for a research, development, or demonstration project. This offer could be a legitimate means by which to provide a candidate with extra funds to cover moving and relocation.

There is always the possibility that no candidates will accept a job offer. Hopefully, the turndowns are not because the department is making the mistake of trying to recruit out of its league or creating negative impressions in the candidates. A study done a number of years ago found candidates turned down job offers at the University of Minnesota for several reasons:

> . . . Apparently then, the rejections were not for the most part due to procedural mismanagement [poor negotiations]. The respondents who stayed in their current positions [N = 58] rejected the appointments primarily because the offers were not enough better in terms of salary, rank, or types of duties to counterbalance the troubles connected with moving to a new institution. Those who accepted alternative offers in preference to Minnesota's [N = 36] reported low salaries, undesirable types of duties or a dislike for the climate or location. . . . [Other undesirable features besides climate were] the lack of provisions for paying moving costs, and the unavailability of suitable housing (Stecklein and Lathrop 1960, p. 37).

Obviously, a rejection of a job offer means the department chair must consider starting the entire process again.

If the candidate does accept the job offer, the chair must make two things clear: first, that a letter will be sent making the formal job offer, to which the candidate should respond promptly and affirmatively, and second, that after some corporate body (board of trustees or board of regents) approves it a contract will be sent (Knowles 1970, II). If a letter of intent to employ is signed by a dean or other college official, the candidate may begin to make plans to move to the new institution, but until the candidate receives the official contract, he is not bound to the new position, nor can he be 100 percent certain of being employed by the new institution. The department chair or head secretary should follow the progress of the paperwork through the institutional bureaucracy and keep the candidate informed. The department head should arrange for one or two faculty members or their spouses to assist the candidate in the identification of desirable residential areas and location of shopping areas. The new faculty member should be encouraged to arrive at the college or university 2 weeks to 1 month before the term begins to give him time to adjust to a new community, a new institution, and a new department.

Terminating the Search

After a search has been completed, notices must be sent to all original applicants. It is important to indicate only that a person was found who best meets the department's requirements. Any comment about the rejected person's capabilities, etc., is liable to so many misinterpretations that protracted communication and even legal action has resulted.

The chair should be thoroughly conversant with the requirements for compiling, submitting, and storing the records of each recruitment effort. Some institutions will not process appointment papers for a new person until the affirmative action file of the search is complete. Generally, a 3-year holding period is sufficient for records of a search. A specific place may be designated for final disposition of these records, and it might be wise to keep a record of the time invested and costs incurred for any recruiting effort (DuVall 1976).

If the search was unsuccessful, it is still necessary to compile a complete set of records. They can be helpful if the search is reopened. At present, it seems necessary to notify each original applicant when a search is reopened, asking each to indicate whether he wishes to remain an applicant.

If the chair and faculty of a department invest the necessary time, the recruitment effort should be successful. The practice of open communication, begun in the institution during the search, now becomes even more important in dealing with the new faculty member.

> *Underlying the suggested guidelines for faculty selection is one basic premise. . . . Both the prospective faculty appointee and the institution have every right to expect that each will make full and complete disclosure of any and all facts which might bear on the applicant's decision to accept or decline appointment to the faculty and the institution's decision to offer employment in the first instance. Lack of candor at the outset has soured many an employment relationship. Calculated initial concealment of matters pertinent to the proposed educational partnership amounts to willful deception and is indefensible. Unintentional nondisclosure, while more often than not the result of oversight, may be just as damaging to the proposed relationship. The matter of candor, it should be stressed, is a two-way street. The institution's failure to make clear all matters pertinent to employment probably is far more common than a comparable omission by the prospective faculty member. Consequently, a determined mutual effort should be made to inform fully the prospective faculty member what will be expected of him (her) and what (s)he can expect from the institution. In such an atmosphere thus created, misunderstanding, disappointment, suspicion, mistrust, and hostility will be hard pressed to thrive (Miner 1973, p. 27).*

The first step to ensuring full disclosure for the new faculty member is to send him any additional materials about the department and institution not already sent, particularly information about work assignments, opportunities for professional development, evaluation criteria, and requirements for notice of nonrenewal of the contract.

Formal Requirements of Employment
The employment contract for a faculty member is an agreement reached between a person and an institution; although it results in an academic appointment, it also results in a legal relationship between employer and employee. The relationship, however, is a special one because the right of the employer to

---

supervise and control details and methods of performance is not expected to be carried out in any ordinary sense. The implementation of such concepts as shared authority and academic freedom dramatically changes the industrial concept of the usual relationship. Even so, the practices of written annual assignment and annual performance review are more common in higher education and are formalizing the employer-employee relationship.

The employer at a college or university is almost always the corporate board of trustees. It may delegate the power to make academic appointments to a president or other officials, but the board retains the basic authority to review, question, and revoke the actions of administrators that it does not approve. This matter is probably more important in public institutions than in private ones. In multicampus institutions with single boards, the delegation of authority over personnel matters to presidents almost constitutes a de facto grant of corporate power as well as authority. In any case, it is the president and the board who bind the institution financially when a contract is signed. Department heads need to understand that they are often authorized only to *begin* negotiations, and that only deans or other administrators may have the authority to make a firm job offer.

A number of other legally recognized relationships emerge when a candidate accepts an offer of employment. They might be called "loyalty provisions." The most obvious kind was the oath that had to be signed by all people accepting public employment (Knowles 1970, II). Florida used to require such an oath and even required all faculty to be fingerprinted. Not many such provisions remain in force, primarily because they have been voluntarily removed or because of a decision by the U.S. Supreme Court, which found that many of their statutory provisions were excessively vague and unwarranted regulations of speech (Knowles 1970, II).

Some church-sponsored (or -related) colleges still require verbal agreement from teachers that they will not interfere with religious activities; a few apparently still require a signed statement from each faculty member to the effect that they support the sponsoring church. Most such institutions are exempt from state and federal laws but only if they receive no funds from the government.

Some state systems of higher education and some institutions, community junior colleges in particular, may require applicants for faculty positions to submit an acceptable statement

of educational philosophy. Whether these statements are anything more than a mere recitation of code words or actually have some demonstrated impact on the educational experience of students has almost never been studied.* They tend to appear like public confessions of faith in organized religion. However, a department or division chair may have to explain their ideological underpinnings to the new faculty member.

The contractual relationship in any organization, college or university included, unless specifically stated otherwise, also involves an assumption of loyalty. The employee is expected to be faithful, honest, and supportive and not to betray the interests of the institution. Colleges and universities can hardly push this matter very hard because external agencies accredit institutions and many of their programs and because faculty win their greatest recognition from their professional disciplinary associations outside the institution. The less cosmopolitan an institution and its faculty, however, the greater may be its ability to make loyalty an issue—through pay, promotion, and other rewards. The department chair must be able to alert the new faculty member to these issues without unduly alarming him or her; explaining a code of ethics for faculty can be very helpful at this time.

Affirmative action, equal pay, and equal employment policies also affect the relationship of a faculty member to the institution. The department chair must be as honest as possible with new faculty about the existence of a "plantation mentality" among administrators and whether any compensating benefits exist in such situations. The new faculty member who is the first woman or minority in a department deserves to know how things get done successfully so that he or she does not become entrapped in destructive conflict. The department head may want to arrange a private counseling session between the new faculty member and other departmental faculty to explain the style of decision making in the college or university.

One often unasked question about affirmative action programs turns out to be more than a hypothetical question at most institutions (Ekstrom 1978): At what point should women and minorities no longer be accorded special advantages because of

*A recent study at a large multicampus community college indicates that faculty can be evaluated as excellent even when they do not subscribe to the traditional hierarchy of often-announced goals for community colleges (Douglas 1982).

past discrimination or underrepresentation? If a woman is recruited and appointed because of her qualifications, is she to be treated as though she was accepted because she is a woman, a qualified woman, or qualified? And how does a chair explain the answer to the faculty and to the new faculty member? Similarly, how does a chair help a woman or minority person understand why he or she was hired but then later not renewed? To hire women and minorities for some reason other than that they were better qualified or at least equal to the other candidates applying for the position is not good policy, nor is it required by affirmative action or equal employment opportunity guidelines.

Formal Orientation and Career Counseling

New faculty members, especially those beginning as instructors or assistant professors, deserve serious attention from the chair and senior faculty. They need a substantial orientation so that they can learn to work effectively very quickly (Knowles 1970, II). They need career guidance from the start and should not be permitted to sink or swim based on a mystical idea that anyone can learn professoring if they will just try. The need for appropriate and insightful guidance of new women and minority faculty members is doubly important. Given the time and effort involved in recruiting, new faculty should not be allowed to fail unless they lack the motivation to acquire the necessary skills and knowledge. Perhaps the greatest attention should be directed to new faculty who are beginning their first full-time appointment (note that this concern is equally applicable to all new faculty, regardless of race and gender.)

One of the first attitudes to be communicated to the new faculty member is that he or she is perceived as a person wanting an active and rewarding career in academe. To achieve it requires the right strategy, a sure understanding of the source of rewards, and a knowledge of the means required to achieve those rewards. A department head can counsel each new faculty member to organize a personal and professional development strategy for success based on the following modes of behavior:

1. Demonstrate dependability. Do whatever is required ahead of time and do it thoroughly.
2. Where a choice of professional activities exists, choose those that provide the best information to build a career

Given the time and effort involved in recruiting, new faculty should not be allowed to fail unless they lack the motivation to acquire the necessary skills and knowledge.

(e.g., identify sources of funding if research and publication are important).

3. Overachieve only on things with "exchange value" (activities that contribute to career goals) and minimize those things with "use value" (regular work assignments).

4. In setting priorities, do those things first that contribute to professional growth; as a bonus, they help develop and demonstrate competence and expertise to colleagues.

5. When outside forces of accountability impinge on professional activities, report it to peers for their response, suggestions, and recommended strategies for coping.

6. Learn the formal and informal institutional rules, understand them, use them to achieve career goals, and attempt to change them if they are hindrances.

7. Manage time; don't get trapped into nurturing and developmental activities beyond those necessary for a reasonable performance of regular assignments.

8. Learn which activities count most in the quest for promotion and tenure; maximize the ones that count most.

9. Be active professionally; establish a broad network of contacts and sources of information; become professionally visible (Gideonse 1981).*

These nine principles seemingly represent the way 48 professors (47 male, 1 female, of all ranks) at a major research university defined their early career activities. "The aspiring professors may not be unwilling to help others but, due to the environmental press to publish and get promoted, are unable to do so at this stage in their career" (Braskamp, Fowler, and Ory 1982, p. 18).

The department head can be especially helpful when a single parent, male or female, is appointed to the department. A single parent (or married woman) often must play multiple roles, requiring schedules to be juggled and arrangements for home and children made and then changed. Eventually, the initial settling-in problems become somewhat routine, but colleagues can ease a new person's adjustment by being tolerant and by offering helpful advice about desirable schools, honest car repair shops, and so on.

*Edited by the author.

Another important problem facing new faculty is the need to break into the informal culture of the department, division, or college. While current faculty may not perceive the Wednesday night poker game or the drink after work as bastions of male decision making, new faculty, women in particular, may find it difficult to become part of this informal network. One way the chair can open up these situations is to schedule more frequent, informal faculty sessions, perhaps as brown-bag lunches. It would be helpful if female faculty had access to a women's center or network so that other faculty and professional women could help them develop the broad set of institutional contacts necessary to build a successful career. A department head could be instrumental in the creation of such a group if one does not exist already within the institution.

The chair can make life more acceptable to women by using joint references (he/she) or neutral references (they) in memoranda or other documents. Faculty need to become aware and consciously combat prevailing sexist mores. To do so, however, the chair must be convinced that the sexual stereotypes of women are incorrect.

One of the most criticized performance characteristics of female faculty is their alleged poor record of research and publication, which is beginning to be seriously studied. A recent study of 29 men and 19 women who survived peer review to the university promotion and tenure committee at Florida State University found substantial differences between men and women.

> First—and most importantly—the average *research assignment of male candidates was 10% higher than that of female candidates. Statistically, sex of the candidates averaged slightly higher research productivity [for] male candidates. Teaching assignments were even more strongly related to sex, which accounted for 21% of all variance in assignments. Female candidates averaged 17% heavier teaching assignments. . . . With generally heavier teaching assignments and less research assignment, it follows that these female candidates probably had less* opportunity *for research.* Any evaluation based upon absolute quantity of research *would necessarily be* biased against female candidates. *The simple adjustment for assignment proposed here seems eminently fair and in fact shows that the rate of research output*

(per unit of assignment) was greater for female candidates (Fletcher and King 1980, p. 12) (emphasis added).

The authors took into account this finding when comparing the rates of research productivity and promotion:

when individual research output (number of publications) was adjusted for opportunity (research assignment), the resulting research productivity was no longer correlated with promotion/tenure recommendations. Indeed, in many cases candidates who were not recommended for promotion/tenure were relatively more productive than were recommended candidates [read "female" in the former, "male" in the latter categories] (Fletcher and King 1980, p. 19).

The votes of the lower-level faculty promotion and tenure committees may have influenced the university committee, and some measure of quality of research or publication could have influenced decisions to grant tenure. Nevertheless, it appeared that "absolute quantity of research output seems to have been the primary determinant of promotion and tenure" (Fletcher and King 1980, p. 19).

This study makes it clear that research and publication depend upon opportunity. For women and other new faculty to be successful in this area, they need large research assignments. Both the department chair and senior faculty need to understand the need for this opportunity. Ofter senior faculty expect, as due their seniority in the department, that they will be given lighter teaching loads. The chair is the one who must take into account not just affirmative action but also a general concern with the retention of new faculty and balance the assignments for teaching and research.

Similarly, special counseling and assignments need to be prepared for each black faculty member newly hired. Both male and female blacks who join the faculties of white institutions are most interested in students and teaching and working in an intellectual atmosphere (Moore and Wagstaff 1974). If devotion to students and teaching will not by themselves bring promotion and tenure, then appropriate additional assignments must be made.

Development Plans for New Faculty

New faculty, those without previous full-time employment in academe, deserve a development plan at the outset of their careers (Lazarus and Tolpin 1979; Medalia 1963). Letting them learn the ropes without any formal guidance is a mistake on two counts: (1) their present skills are based on learning and imitation, which likely as not include as many wrong ways as right ways to function effectively (Sawyer 1974); (2) a new faculty member needs to become competent in at least four areas—teaching, research, advising students, and service. It is the department head's responsibility to develop a plan and simple indicators of successful performance for each competency (Lazarus and Tolpin 1979)—the quality of mind to develop new perspectives and present them openmindedly and enthusiastically to students (Florida Board of Regents 1971), knowledge of the institution's degree programs coupled with the ability to transmit accurate information to students, and service to the community, state, and nation by fully applying one's competence in professional associations. The departmental faculty must agree to the proposed criteria for indicators of success and to the weight that should be given each in evaluating new faculty (Tucker 1981). These items need to be spelled out in the annual and term assignments made for each new faculty member, especially during the first few years.

The chair may find it appropriate to form a small committee to review the progress of each new faculty member; it could meet quarterly or more often. If the chair is male and the new faculty member is female and/or a minority, then it would be helpful to have such a person on the committee even if he or she must come from another department. Forming a League of Mentors, who can help junior faculty, especially minorities and women, is another means for helping these people to survive, thrive, and succeed (Peck 1982).

The department chair's ability to converse openly with minorities and women about their career development is very important. In a study of large corporations, however, male supervisors often would not counsel or confront women because "they thought they'd break down in the office and cry" (Collins 1982, p. C1). The researcher who conducted the study discovered "that most of the men and women didn't have one strong mentor figure to help them" (Collins 1982, p. C1). They all agreed about the importance of a mentor, but most did not have one. Most new faculty would probably report the same experience.

A department chair, even if male, *must* know how to steer a new female faculty member to a woman's network on campus. In a study of job satisfaction among women professors in 20 Pennsylvania institutions of higher education, it appeared that women faculty are more satisfied in institutions with a faculty having at least 20 percent women, particularly among the youngest age group studied (25–35)(Hill 1982). Overall satisfaction was also

> *more pronounced among humanities, social and behavioral science, social service, and mathematics and physical science faculty; and among these groups the economic dimension is often the most significantly affected dimension of job satisfaction (Hill 1982, p. 17).*

Hill concludes that his tentative findings suggest the need of a support network, particularly at the institutions where more women faculty are employed.

The idea of a support network might include the concept of a League of Mentors to help the new faculty member grow professionally. The concept of a mentor for beginning faculty must be clarified, however, because the recent graduate student may often already have a mentor.

> *Mentorship is widely regarded as an important aspect of the training and career development of young professionals. . . . Within the academic profession mentorship most often occurs in the informal, but special sponsorship that a graduate student receives from a senior professor during graduate school. The mentor provides a role model, academic advice, and eventually, assistance in gaining access to the profession. . . . The career/success of young faculty [is] significantly influenced by the quality of the institution in which they [find] employment and the extent of their collaboration with senior faculty. Moreover, the type and quality of the institution where they [find] employment [is] closely tied to the professional contacts and associations of the mentor (Blackburn, Chapman, and Cameron 1981, p. 315).*

The department or division chair who actively participates in the negotiations to hire a new faculty member has a special opportunity to act as a surrogate mentor. However, a role conflict may develop when the chair must also evaluate the person's performance. Perhaps the surrogate mentor could come from among the faculty within or without the department.

Why Do Faculty Leave Voluntarily?

In spite of many serious efforts to retain faculty, some will move anyway (Hall 1977). Reasons vary: the perception that tenure will not be granted; better opportunities for professional advancement and responsibilities at another institution; better salary, research support, travel funds, and availability of student assistants at another institution; personal reasons having to do with proximity to relatives, good schools for children, life at a slower pace in a small town; the perceived attitudes and procedures of a department administrator. (See Caplow and McGee 1958 and Stecklein and Lathrop 1960 for studies of reasons why faculty leave positions.) Interestingly, Stecklein and Lathrop (1960) found that of faculty receiving job offers who decided to *stay*, 69 percent mentioned their good relations with colleagues and administrators, beginning with department heads.

Thus, department chairs who want to build a stable and productive departmental faculty need also to examine themselves and their relationship with their colleagues. The faculty in the Stecklein and Lathrop study who left the university recommended that the department chair improve communications with the younger faculty to make sure they were informed about possibilities for their promotion and tenure and that the chairs indicate some interest in the work of the younger faculty. Women faculty at the 1981 annual meeting of the American Education Research Association expressed the same need. Open communication is apparently crucial for department chairs and for any college or university that wants to build and retain a quality faculty.

Black educators leave for somewhat different reasons. In one survey, some of those who left the predominantly white colleges and universities to which they had been recruited, moved to traditionally black institutions; others questioned their fair treatment in comparison with their white colleagues (Moore and Wagstaff 1974, p. 136). A minority (less than 25 percent left for an increase in salary (p. 139). However, being black in a white institution may itself have created the kinds of tensions and anxieties in some black faculty that caused them to leave

Department chairs who want to build a stable and productive departmental faculty need also to examine themselves and their relationship with their colleagues.

(p. 139). It seems clear that to recruit black faculty to a white institution creates a responsibility to help them adapt to the white institution. The department chair must work to root out racist institutional practices, in addition to supplying guidance and assistance to new minority faculty.

SUMMARY

The role of the department head is crucial in making fair recruitment work. Openness, a willingness to confront preconceptions and a commitment to equality and quality can change the way a department conducts its affairs. A dedicated chair can lead a department to this mature level of decision making.

But the constraints of frugality, open competitiveness to survive, and fear of unfair evaluations can dry up cooperation. The chair has a special opportunity to recharge a department when a position becomes vacant. A department's goals and priorities can be reexamined when a position description is reviewed and written. The curriculum, often full of vested interests, can be revised for relevance and quality. Faculty assignments can be shifted and some intellectual vigor stimulated through new course assignments. With a department head's leadership, the life of the mind can regain some vigor.

American higher education has had a unique responsibility not given to any other sector of society to recognize and nurture talent. Over the past few decades, it has become evident that most of this important activity occurred because the talent often sought the faculty. Now it has become evident that some of the best of the several kinds of talent may go unnoticed. The search must be extended, intellect identified wherever it exists, and talent sought in places where it normally is not sought. Too often we cry because the intellect is not respected; perhaps it is not respected because we do not pursue it like the football coach who creates value in the intense pursuit of the potential star athlete. To take what comes our way is to ride with the tide; to pursue excellence or its potential is to sail across the wind, a challenging tack for any departmental captain.

BIBLIOGRAPHY

The ERIC Clearinghouse on Higher Education abstracts and indexes the current literature on higher education for the National Institute of Education's monthly bibliographic journal *Resources in Education*. Most of these publications are available through the ERIC Document Reproduction Service (EDRS). For publications cited in this bibliography that are available from EDRS, ordering number and price are included. Readers who wish to order a publication should write to the ERIC Document Reproduction Service, P.O. Box 190, Arlington, Virginia 22210. When ordering, please specify the document number. Documents are available as noted in microfiche (MF) and paper copy (PC).

"ACE Defends Equal Opportunity, Backs Deregulation." *Higher Education and National Affairs* 30 (Nov. 6, 1981):3.

"ACE Recommends Rule Changes for U.S. Contractors to Achieve Equality Goals." *Higher Education and National Affairs* 30 (Nov. 6, 1981):3–4.

"Affirmative Action Called 'Vandalism' in Committee Hearing." *Higher Education and National Affairs* 30 (June 19, 1981):3.

Association of Governing Boards of Universities and Colleges. *Gateways and Barriers for Women in the University Community*. Washington, D.C.: Association of Governing Boards, 1977. ED 139 357. MF–$1.17; PC–$11.08.

Bayer, Alan E., and Astin, Helen S. "Sex Differentials in the Academic Reward System." *Science* 188 (1975):796–802.

Blackburn, Robert T.; Chapman, David W.; and Cameron, Susan M. " 'Cloning' in Academe: Mentorship and Academic Careers." *Research in Higher Education* 15 (1981):315–27.

Braithwaite, Ronald L., and Beatty, Lula. "Minority Male Participation in Educational Research and Development: A Recruitment Selection Dilemma." *Journal of Negro Education* 50 (Fall 1981):389–400.

Braskamp, Larry A.; Fowler, Deborah L.; and Ory, John C. "Faculty Development and Achievement: A Faculty's View." Paper presented at the Annual Meeting of the American Educational Research Association, March 1982, in New York City. ED 216 626. MF–$1.17; PC–$5.45.

Bunzel, John H. "To Each According to Her Worth?" *The Public Interest* 67 (Spring 1982):77–93.

Butterfield, Fox. "Falsifying of College Records by Job Seekers Found on Rise." *New York Times* (Nov. 29, 1981):1.

Caplow, Theodore, and McGee, Reece J. *The Academic Marketplace*. Garden City, N.Y.: Anchor Books, 1958.

Carnegie Council on Policy Studies in Higher Education. *Making Affirmative Action Work in Higher Education: An Analysis of Institu-*

tional and Federal Policies with Recommendations. San Francisco: Jossey-Bass, 1975.

Carroll, Mary R., and Clark, David L. *Women in Colleges and Universities: Equity for Women in Higher Education Project.* Bloomington, Ind.: Indiana University, and Columbus, Ohio: University Council for Educational Administration, 1978. ED 198 762. MF–$1.17; PC–$9.33.

Collins, Glenn. "You've Come a Long Way, Lady, but You Ain't There Yet." *Tallahassee Democrat* (June 2, 1982):C1.

Commission on Civil Rights. *Affirmative Action in Employment in Higher Education.* Washington, D.C.: U.S. Commission on Civil Rights, 1975. ED 144 518. MF–$1.17; PC–$20.60.

Cosper, Wilma. "Nepotism: Desirable or Undesirable?" *Improving College and University Teaching* 18 (Autumn 1970):282–84.

Crane, Diane. "The Academic Marketplace Revisited: A Study of Faculty Mobility Using the Cartter Ratings." *American Journal of Sociology* 75 (May 1970):953–63.

"Differing Perspectives on Declining Faculty Salaries." *Current Issues in Higher Education* 2 (Sept. 17, 1980):1–20.

Douglas, Ruth. "Faculty Attitudes toward Community College Goals Compared with the Perceived Effectiveness of Faculty Professional Activities at Northern Virginia Community College." Ph.D. dissertation, Florida State University, 1982.

DuVall, Charles R. *A Cost Study of the Activities of a Selected Search and Screen Committee.* South Bend, Ind.: Indiana University at South Bend, 1976. ED 126 800. MF–$1.17; PC–$3.70.

Ekstrom, Ruth B. *Issues in the Recruitment, Professional Development, Promotion, and Remuneration of Women Faculty.* Princeton, N.J.: Educational Testing Service, 1978. ED 161 318. MF–$1.17; PC not available EDRS.

"Equal Pay Principle Expanded." *Atlanta Constitution* (June 9, 1981):1.

"The Erosion of Academe." *UFF Reach* 1 (Winter 1980):6–19.

Fernandez, Luis. *U.S. Faculty after the Boom: Demographic Projections to 2000.* Berkeley, Cal.: Carnegie Council on Policy Studies in Higher Education, 1978. ED 165 618. MF–$1.17; PC–$16.72.

Fishel, Andrew, and Pottker, Janice. *National Politics and Sex Discrimination in Education.* Lexington, Mass.: Lexington Books, 1977.

Fleming, John E.; Gill, Gerald R.; and Swinton, David L. *The Case for Affirmative Action for Blacks in Higher Education.* Washington, D.C.: Howard University Press, 1978.

Fletcher, Harold J., and King, Thomas R. "Promotion and Tenure at Florida State University 1979–1980: The Candidates and the Recommendations of the University Committee." Photocopied. Tallahassee: Florida State University, Department of Educational

Research, Development, and Foundations, 1980. Florida Board of Regents. "A Position Paper on Faculty Selection, Development, Evaluation, and Retention." Offset Tallahassee: Board of Regents, 1971.

Florida Department of Education. *Legal Implications of Faculty Selection, Development, Evaluation, and Retention.* Tallahassee: Florida Department of Education, Division of Community Colleges, 1973.

Florida State University. *A Resource Document for Implementing Recruitment of Minorities and Women at the Florida State University.* Tallahassee: Florida State University, 1973. ED 109 968. MF– $1.17; PC–$12.83.

Florida State University. *Handbook for Search and Screening Committees.* Tallahassee: Florida State University, University Human Affairs Office, 1980.

Fortunato, Ray T., and Waddell, D. Geneva. *Personnel Administration in Higher Education.* San Francisco: Jossey-Bass, 1981.

Gaddy, Dale. *Faculty Recruitment.* Washington, D.C.: American Association of Junior Colleges, 1969. ED 032 864. MF–$1.17; PC– $3.70.

Gideonse, Hendrik D. "Power Strategies for the Advancement of Academic Women." Summary presented at the Annual Meeting of the American Educational Research Association, 15 April 1981, in New York City.

Greenhouse, Linda. "Court Says School Anti-Bias Rules Cover Workers as Well as Pupils." *New York Times* (May 18, 1982):1.

———. "Equal Pay Debate Now Shifts to a Far Wider Concept." *New York Times* (March 22, 1981):18E.

Haber, B. "Why Not the Best and the Brightest? Equal Opportunity versus Academic Freedom." *Equal Opportunity Forum* 8 (Oct. 1981): 11–15.

Hall, Robert N., ed. *A Symposium on Faculty Retention, Tenure, Promotion, and Graduate Department Evaluation.* Report presented at Speech Communication Association, April 1977. ED 144 110. MF–$1.17; PC not available EDRS.

Hechinger, Fred M. "A Lost Generation of Young 'Gypsy Scholars.'" *New York Times* (May 2, 1982): EY21.

Heim, Peggy. "The Economic Decline of the Professoriate in the 80's: What Happened to Faculty Salaries and What Are the Implications?"*Current Issues in Higher Education* 3 (1980): 12–20. ED 194 006. MF–$1.17; PC not available EDRS.

Hill, Malcolm D. "Faculty Sex Composition and Job Satisfaction among Academic Women." Paper presented at the Annual Meeting of the American Educational Research Association, March 1982, in New York City. ED 215 632. MF–$1.17; PC not available EDRS.

Hornig, Lilli S. "HERStory." *Grants Magazine* 1 (March 1978): 1, 36–42.

Hunt, Morton. "A Fraud That Shook the World of Science." *New York Times Magazine* (Nov. 1, 1981):42–46.

King, Charles W. "Improving the Academic Level of Church College Faculty." *Improving College and University Teaching* 24 (Autumn 1976): 219–20.

Knowles, Asa S., ed. *Handbook of College and University Administration.* Vol. 1, *General* and Vol. 2, *Academic*. New York: McGraw-Hill, 1970.

Koch, James V., and Chizmar, John F., Jr. *The Economics of Affirmative Action.* Lexington, Mass.: Lexington Books, 1976.

Lawrence, Susan. "Watching the Watchers." *Science News* 119 (1981): 331–34.

Lazarus, Barbara, and Tolpin, Martha. "Engaging Junior Faculty in Career Planning: Alternatives to the Exit Interview." *Current Issues in Higher Education* 2 (1979): 29–32. ED 193 998. MF–$1.17; PC not available EDRS.

Lewin, Arie Y., and Duchan, Linda. "Women in Academia: A Study of the Hiring Decision in Departments of Physical Science." *Science* 173 (1971): 892–95.

Lewis, Lionel S. "The University and the Professional Model: Amplification on a Magnification." *American Behavior Scientist* 14 (1971): 541–62.

Linnell, Robert H. "Age, Sex, and Ethnic Trade-Offs in Faculty Employment: You Can't Have Your Cake and Eat It Too." *Current Issues in Higher Education* 4 (1979). ED 194 000. MF–$1.17; PC not available EDRS.

Lovett, Clara M. "The Job Crisis as an Opportunity: Reflections of an Academic Humanist." Paper presented at the National Conference on Higher Education, 5 March 1981, at Washington, D.C. Offset.

Marcus, Laurence R. "Has Advertising Produced Results in Faculty Hiring?" *Educational Record* 57 (1977): 247–50.

McKeachie, Wilbert J. "Memo to New Department Chairmen." In *The Academic Department or Division Chairman: A Complex Role*, edited by James Brann and Thomas Emmett. Detroit: Balamp, 1972.

Medalia, N. Z. *On Becoming a College Teacher: A Review of Three Variables.* SREB Research Monograph No. 6. Atlanta: Southern Regional Education Board, 1963. ED 149 660. MF–$1.17; PC–$5.45.

Miller, Michael H. "Academic Inbreeding in Nursing." *Nursing Outlook* 25 (1977): 172–77.

Miner, Charles E., Jr. "Legal Considerations in the Selection and Termination Stages of Employment: Challenge for Department/Division Chairmen." In *First-Level Management: Legal Implications and Responsibilities for Selection and Retention of Faculty.* Tallahassee: Florida State University, Department of Higher Education, 1973. ED 073 758. MF–$1.17; PC–$7.20.

Mitchell, Joyce M., and Starr, Rachel R. "A Regional Approach for Analyzing the Recruitment of Academic Women." *American Behavioral Scientist* 15 (1971): 183–205.

Mohl, Bruce A. "Age-bias Lawsuits May Provide Answer to a Puzzle." *Florida Times-Union* (June 13, 1982): F1.

Moore, William, Jr., and Wagstaff, Lonnie H. *Black Educators in White Colleges.* San Francisco: Jossey-Bass, 1974.

National Science Foundation. "Tenure Practices in Universities and 4-Year Colleges Affect Faculty Turnover." *Science Resources Studies Highlights.* Washington, D.C.: NSF Division of Science Resources Studies, 1981. ED 200 126. MF–$1.17; PC not available EDRS.

Nelson, Bryce. "Job Applicants: How They Lie about Their Past." *Los Angeles Times* (April 17, 1981): B1.

Palley, Marian L., and Preston, Michael B., eds. *Race, Sex, and Policy Problems.* Lexington, Mass.: Lexington Books, 1979.

Pear, Robert. "Courts and Lawmakers Restoring Intent as Ground for Proof of Bias." *New York Times* (April 19, 1981): 1.

Peck, Jon. "Educators Organize Mentor League at FSU." *Florida Times-Union* (Sept. 15, 1982): B2.

Pinegree, Suzanne, et al. "Anti-Nepotism's Ghost: Attitudes of Administrators toward Hiring Professional Couples." *Psychology of Women Quarterly* 3 (Fall 1978): 23–29.

Poort, Stephen M. *Guidelines for the Recruitment and Selection of Community College Faculty.* Gainesville, Fla.: University of Florida, Institute of Higher Education, 1971. ED 058 868. MF–$1.17; PC–$5.45.

Prather, Jane. "Why Can't Women Be More Like Men: A Summary of the Sociopsychological Factors Hindering Women's Advancement in the Professions." *American Behavioral Scientist* 15 (1971): 172–82.

President's Council. "Part-Time Faculty: A Position Paper." Attachment 4 to the Minutes of the Community College President's Council. Tallahassee: Florida Department of Education, Division of Community Colleges, 1980.

Radner, Roy, and Kuh, Charlotte V. *Preserving a Lost Generation: Policies to Assure a Steady Flow of Young Scholars until the Year 2000. A Report and Recommendations.* Berkeley, Cal.: Carnegie Council on Policy Studies in Higher Education, 1978. ED 165 575. MF–$1.17; PC–$7.20.

Rood, Harold J. "Legal Issues in Faculty Termination." *Journal of Higher Education* 63 (1977): 123–52.

Roper, Dwight. "The Waning of the Old Boy Network: Placement, Publishing, and Faculty Selection." *Improving College and University Teaching* 28 (Winter 1980): 12–18.

Ross, Ronald D. "The Fine Art of Faculty Recruitment." *Music Education Journal* 67 (May 1981): 49–51.

Russell, Richard. "The Plight of the 'Part-Time, Adjunct Ad Hoc' Teacher." *UFF Reach* 1 (Winter 1980): 13.

Sandler, Bernice Resnick. "You've Come a Long Way, Maybe—Or Why It Still Hurts to Be a Woman in Labor." *Current Issues in Higher Education* 4 (1979): 11–14. ED 194 000. MF–$1.17; PC not available EDRS.

Sawyer, Paul. "The Presentation: Testing Potential New Faculty's Ability to Teach." *AAUP Bulletin* 60 (1974): 379–80.

Schmuck, Patricia A., ed. *Educational Policy and Management: Sex Differentials.* New York: Academic Press, 1981.

Schumer, Fran R. "A Question of Sex Bias at Harvard." *New York Times Magazine* (Oct. 18, 1981): 96–100.

Seyfried, Shirley H., et al. "Factors Influencing Faculty Choice of Position." *Nursing Outlook* 25 (1977): 692–96.

Shulman, Carol H. *Affirmative Action: Women's Rights on Campus.* Washington, D.C.: American Association for Higher Education, 1972. ED 066 143. MF–$1.17; PC–$5.45.

Smelser, Neil J., and Content, Robin. *The Changing Academic Market: General Trends and a Berkeley Case Study.* Berkeley, Cal.: University of California Press, 1980.

Sommerfield, Richard, and Nagely, Donna. "Seek and Ye Shall Find: The Organization and Conduct of a Search Committee." *Journal of Higher Education* 45 (April 1974): 239–52.

Sowell, Thomas. *Ethnic America: A History.* New York: Basic Books, 1981.

———. *Markets and Minorities.* New York: Basic Books, 1982.

State of Florida. *Florida's Commitment to Equal Access and Equal Opportunity in Public Higher Education.* Tallahassee: State University System and Division of Community Colleges, 1978. ED 167 678. MF–$1.17; PC not available EDRS.

Stecklein, John E., and Lathrop, Robert L. *Faculty Attraction and Retention.* Minneapolis: University of Minnesota, Bureau of Institutional Research, 1960.

Strohm, Paul. "Faculty Search Committees and Review Committees: What to Do until the Bargaining Agent Comes." *AAUP Bulletin* 60 (1974): 288–90.

Tucker, Allan. *Chairing the Academic Department: Leadership among Peers.* Washington, D.C.: American Council on Education, 1981.

Vetter, Betty M. "More Women for Higher Education." *Science* 178 (1972): 815.

"Why Women Ph.D's Advance More Slowly." *Science News* 120 (1981): 294.

Wolotkiewicz, Rita J. *College Administrators' Handbook.* Boston: Allyn & Bacon, 1980.

Yarrow, Andrew. "Gypsy Scholars Roam Academic Landscape." *New York Times* (Jan. 10, 1982): 13, education section.

ASHE-ERIC Higher Education Research Reports

Starting in 1983 the Association for the Study of Higher Education assumed co-sponsorship of the Higher Education Research Reports with the ERIC Clearinghouse on Higher Education. For the previous eleven years ERIC and the American Association for Higher Education prepared and published the reports.

Each report is the definitive analysis of a tough higher education problem, based on a thorough research of pertinent literature and institutional experiences. Report topics, identified by a national survey, are written by noted practitioners and scholars with pre-publication manuscript reviews by experts.

Ten monographs in the ASHE-ERIC/Higher Education Research Report series are published each year, available individually or by subscription. Subscription to 10 issues is $50 regular; $35 for members of AERA, AAHE, and AIR; $30 for members of ASHE. (Add $7.50 outside U.S.).

Prices for single copies, including 4th class postage and handling, are $6.50 regular and $5.00 for members of AERA, AAHE, AIR, and ASHE. If faster first-class postage is desired for U.S. and Canadian orders, add $.60; for overseas, add $4.50. For VISA and Mastercharge payments, give card number, expiration date and signature. Orders under $25 must be prepaid. Bulk discounts are available on orders of 25 or more of a single title. Order from the Publications Department, Association for the Study of Higher Education, One Dupont Circle, Suite 630, Washington, D.C. 20036, (202) 296-2597. Write for a complete list of Higher Education Research Reports and other ASHE and ERIC publications.

1981 Higher Education Research Reports

1. Minority Access to Higher Education
   Jean L. Preer

2. Institutional Advancement Strategies in Hard Times
   Michael D. Richards and Gerald Sherratt

3. Functional Literacy in the College Setting
   Richard C. Richardson, Jr., Kathryn J. Martens, and Elizabeth C. Fisk

4. Indices of Quality in the Undergraduate Experience
   George D. Kuh

5. Marketing in Higher Education
   Stanley M. Grabowski

6. Computer Literacy in Higher Education
   Francis E. Masat

7. Financial Analysis for Academic Units
   Donald L. Walters

8. Assessing the Impact of Faculty Collective Bargaining
   J. Victor Baldridge, Frank K. Kemerer, and Associates

9. Strategic Planning, Management and Decision Making
   Robert G. Cope
10. Organizational Communication in Higher Education
    Robert D. Gratz and Philip J. Salem

1982 Higher Education Research Reports

1. Rating College Teaching: Criterion Studies of Student Evaluation-of-Instruction Instruments
   Sidney E. Benton
2. Faculty Evaluation: The Use of Explicit Criteria for Promotion, Retention, and Tenure
   Neal Whitman and Elaine Weiss
3. The Enrollment Crisis: Factors, Actors, and Impacts
   J. Victor Baldridge, Frank R. Kemerer, and Kenneth C. Green
4. Improving Instruction: Issues and Alternatives for Higher Education
   Charles C. Cole, Jr.
5. Planning for Program Discontinuance: From Default to Design
   Gerlinda S. Melchiori
6. State Planning, Budgeting, and Accountability: Approaches for Higher Education
   Carol E. Floyd
7. The Process of Change in Higher Education Institutions
   Robert C. Nordvall
8. Information Systems and Technological Decisions: A Guide for Non-Technical Administrators
   Robert L. Bailey
9. Government Support for Minority Participation in Higher Education
   Kenneth C. Green
10. The Department Chair: Professional Development and Role Conflict
    David B. Booth

1983 Higher Education Research Reports

1. The Path to Excellence: Quality Assurance in Higher Education
   Laurence R. Marcus, Anita O. Leone, and Edward Goldberg

2. Faculty Recruitment, Retention, and Fair Employment: Obligations and Opportunities
   John S. Waggaman